W9-DGK-623

POCKET
INTERNET

The
Economist
Books

POCKET

INTERNET

SEAN GEER

THE ECONOMIST IN ASSOCIATION WITH
PROFILE BOOKS LTD

Profile Books Ltd
58A Hatton Garden, London EC1N 8LX
www.profilebooks.co.uk

Published by Profile Books Ltd
in association with
The Economist Newspaper Ltd 2000

Consultant editor   Oliver Morton
Website research   Kate Galbraith, Paul Pedley

Typest in Garamond by MacGuru
info@macguru.org.uk

Printed in Italy by
LEGO S.p.a. – Vicenza – Italy

A CIP catalogue record for this book is available
from the British Library

ISBN 1 86197 260 1

CONTENTS

PREFACE

As the contents list on the previous page makes clear, this book is arranged in three sections. It begins with essays on key issues. Next comes an A–Z of terms and jargon in which SMALL CAPITALS are used to indicate a cross reference. Last come a series of appendices ranging from a brief history of the Internet to websites recommended by those who work for or read *The Economist*.

If you have any comments or suggestions about anything in the book please send them to the publisher at info@profilebooks.co.uk

INTRODUCTION

Dolly Parton, a popular singer, once remarked "you'd be surprised how much it cost to look this cheap". It's a sentiment that will strike a chord with Internet users, bewitched by the astronomical sums being invested in and raised by new Internet startups but bewildered by the rawness and anarchy of the medium. Something with that much money sloshing about it should, we think, be a bit easier to use, a bit more robust and – dare we say it – a bit classier too.

The purpose of this book is to help the reader understand why the Internet is the way it is, both immensely useful – for many people the easiest way to find out where your nearest harpsichord teacher lives, which metro station serves the Louvre or what to eat if you want more vitamin E – and immensely frustrating. Reaction to the first edition of *Pocket Internet* underlined how significant the Internet has become. This second edition includes a lot of new or revised material about this incredibly fast-moving "thing". In it you will find the technological terms explained, the business ideas analysed, the more relevant parts of the medium's short history laid out and some of its startling statistics presented. It is meant to serve as a companion to anyone trying to make sense of the new medium, its potential and its pitfalls. From Java to junk e-mail, from server to source code, it's here.

The Internet is not just a store of arcane information and a medium for e-mail; it's a social invention capable of endlessly reinventing itself, and in the process driving change throughout the world. Parvenu electronic stockbrokers become worth more than their decades-old antecedents overnight, and do nearly as much business with a whole new type of client. A single film fan in Austin, Texas, can become a Hollywood word-of-mouth expert by putting all the people who queue for sneak previews in touch with each other. Protest groups can synchronise their actions around the world just as businesses do. And it all happens incredibly fast. In 1995 about 10m Americans were online; by the end of 2000 it is estimated that the total will be around 137m – about half of the population. The rest of the world is following suit.

At some point things will slow down; but not yet. For the time being, the dizzying numbers that make up the Internet economy will continue to grow, much faster than a book like this one can ever keep up with them. But there is no danger of the technology failing to keep up, simply because the technology that runs the Internet – much of which you will find explained between these covers – is old and proven. The driver for change is people. The more people start using the net, the more things it will be used for. That simple fact underlies all the sometimes tatty, sometimes breath-taking Internet hoopla. If it can be turned into data, the Internet is the most far-reaching way there is of moving it around – whatever "it" may be.

Sean Geer
July 2000

Part 1

ESSAYS

THE INFORMATION SOCIETY

The realisation that computers are as useful for communicating as they are for calculating and doing other clever things was a long time in coming. The focus on productivity in the workplace and the development of new graphical user interfaces such as Windows have for years reinforced the idea of computers as tools for getting jobs done, not for talking to other people. But it is its ability to connect people together in new and almost limitlessly inventive ways that has formed the basis of the Internet's astonishing growth. Much more than just a vast network of wires and computers, the Internet has emerged as a medium for discussion, business and invention that is busily turning our society on its head.

Perhaps understandably, it still takes a considerable leap of faith for people to accept that light bulbs, say, or lawnmowers might benefit from being woven into new, intelligent networks – even though they might. But almost everyone understands the value of people being connected together. In particular, the power of e-mail – so evident to the academic and corporate users of the last two decades – has become abundantly clear to anyone who has received a message from an overseas colleague, a distant family member or a forgotten friend. Its asynchronous nature, and the freedom this brings from time zones, busy telephone lines and intimidating voice-mail devices, has ensured that e-mail has become the Internet's "killer app", the element of the medium that has proved instrumental in persuading hundreds of millions of people of its broader usefulness and range.

The extent of e-mail's impact can be neatly gauged from a glance at the number of web-based e-mail accounts. Services like Hotmail, Microsoft's free web-based product, have exploded. Travellers use it to stay in touch with families, office workers use it for personal e-mail, grandparents depend on it for contacting grandchildren and technology professionals rely on it for back-up. Hotmail alone claimed nearly 60m accounts in March 2000, a reflection of the fact that people really do want to communicate all the time, irrespective of who or where they are.

And communicate they do, not just by e-mail but with an ever-expanding array of community-building tools and websites. In the United States, the fastest-growing group of web users is not the grungy 20-somethings that characterised its early years but the so-called silver surfers aged over 50. Young people, too, have adopted Internet technology enthusiastically, as a way of planning their busy social lives and extending their entertainment sources way beyond the television or video game console. It is unsurprising, if occasionally humbling for parents, that children should have taken to Internet technology so readily. They have, after all, been programming video recorders and installing Playstations for years. It is perhaps more surprising that people should be using it to recruit vicars, as happened in a village in the UK that, until a young parishioner put out an appeal on the net, could not fill its vacancy. But that merely helped to confirm what those in the know – netheads, digerati, call them what you will – have understood for several years: the Internet is technology for everyone, everywhere, all the time. Whether you need a new vicar, a new submarine or a new recipe for Christmas cake, the Internet can help you find it.

Inevitably, the ready availability of so much information, and the growing enthusiasm with which adults and children now seek it out, has created problems and has brought the issue of censorship to the fore. Pornography is available in many forms and in many locations on the Internet, often for free. There are recipes not just for cakes but for drugs and bombs too.

Making sense of censorship

Discussions among governments have failed to produce agreement on what threats the Internet presents, let alone how to tackle them. Unsure exactly what the net really is, different countries are looking at different ways of controlling Internet content. Australia, for example, has handed responsibility for controlling indecent or offensive material to its conservative-minded national broadcasting authority, fuelling fears that websites with marginally controversial contents might be shut down to be on the safe side.

But the Internet is not really like other broadcast media. For one thing, if you want information you must generally go and look for it, rather than just have it beamed into your home. For another, while there were once real practical limits to the amount of traffic that broadcast frequenices could handle, which was part of the justification for government control over who got to say what, on the Internet there are hardly any such limits. Perhaps most importantly, it cannot be "switched off" in the same way as a television or radio station. So why place its governance in the hands of broadcasters? Equally, why hold ISPs responsible for the content of messages but not the post office, or the telephone company? Some of these questions have been at least partially answered in America, where ISPs are now granted "common carrier" status and their responsibility for the information is akin to that of the telephone companies and postal services. In the UK, however, recent court cases have determined that ISPs are responsible for the information they carry, despite the fact that they carry it unedited, unmoderated and usually unseen by themselves. Such unlimited liability could undermine the UK's net infrastructure, with serious economic consequences. These issues, and others like them, are important and enduring ones. Although media hysteria over pornography and the Internet has subsided somewhat, the debate over how and whether to censor the Internet is still played out endlessly on television and radio all over the world. Fuelled by reports of its use in high-profile crimes (such as the Brixton and Soho bombings in London in 1999, the perpetrator of which said he had got his bomb-making know how from the Internet), politicians and media commentators have become ever more vocal in their assertions that the Net is a powerful influence on citizens' behaviour, rather than merely a reflection of it.

Courts and constitutions have regularly thwarted would-be censors. In the United States, for example, the Communications Decency Act of 1996 (designed to restrict the transmission of any kind of so-called obscene content) was ruled unconstitutional by the Supreme Court in 1997, on the grounds that it violated the First Amendment principles of free speech.

Those who feel that the Internet offers opportunities rather than threats say that the pro-censorship lobby simply misunderstands the technology and its dynamic effects. But even if the censors win the argument for well-meaning reasons, the technology may defeat them. Internet traffic now exceeds that of the telephone networks in most Western countries. This, allied to the ever-burgeoning number of web pages – well over 1 billion at the beginning of 2000 – will almost certainly make censorship too difficult to achieve. Even Singapore's government has been forced to recognise that for every site it blocks there are hundreds more that it cannot control. As if all this was not enough, another equally taxing problem has appeared.

Hide and seek
Governments cannot control material that they cannot see. This has made them extremely nervous about digital encryption, which allows individuals to conceal the contents of their personal communications so securely that they are to all intents and purposes permanently invisible. Such strong encryption turns the Internet into a playground for drug dealers, pornographers and terrorists, according to its opponents, and they want it stopped. The means they plan to use to stop it vary widely. For many years, the US government treated encryption software as munitions, banning its export under the ITAR regulations on arms control. Many of these restrictions are now being

relaxed as the American authorities recognise the importance of security and privacy to the burgeoning world of e-commerce. In the UK, however, the Regulation of Investigatory Powers Bill, scheduled to become law in late 2000, was drafted to allow government agencies to eavesdrop on any kind of electronic conversation. Although it looked as though the government would amend the bill to take into account at least some of the widespread criticism of it, as drafted it would have the effect of forcing ISPs to install costly monitoring equipment to keep tabs on which websites are visited, what goods are bought and what e-mail is received. Furthermore, it would allow for businesses and consumers to be forced to surrender any electronic "keys" that protect their data, with the threat of stiff penalties (including imprisonment) for anyone who refuses to do so.

Ironically, the people such legislation seeks to inconvenience are unlikely to pay it much attention. To paraphrase an old net proverb, outlaw encryption and only outlaws will use it, while the rest of the population will have its confidence undermined in net communications in general and e-commerce in particular. Without security, privacy and freedom to exchange information across global boundaries, the new generation of e-businesses may find their development stifled. This cannot be in any country's economic interest.

BANDWIDTH AND BEYOND

However determined governments are to regulate the behaviour of Internet users, their task will grow exponentially harder as the number of people going online grows dramatically. An estimated 350m people will be online by the end of 2000 and well over twice that number by 2005, nearly half of them in Europe. At the same time, the services these users demand will grow ever more complex, placing pressure on Internet providers and telephone companies to expand not just the volume they can handle but also the amount of data they can exchange efficiently. Accordingly, great changes are going on behind the scenes in the world's telephone exchanges, as bandwidth providers struggle to keep up with the demand.

Rattle those POTS and PANS

After many years of reliable service, POTS, or plain old telephone service, is approaching the end of its useful life as a way of connecting to the Internet. As millions of dial-up subscribers are finding out, the bandwidth demands imposed by modern websites and other information sources are increasing as browsers discover the attractions of modern Java-enabled applications, audio and video. To take full advantage of next-generation Internet applications, such as video on demand, downloadable music, interactive online encyclopedias and complex business-to-business transactions, consumers and companies are looking to new technologies (sometimes referred to as PANS, for Pretty Amazing Network Services) for extra bandwidth.

ADSL (Asymmetric Digital Subscriber Line) is being touted by many carriers as the logical progression from POTS and ISDN for both consumers and business. One of ADSL's great advantages is that it runs across the standard copper wires of the existing local loop, limiting the amount of extra equipment needed to run it to a specialised modem. Typically, an ADSL connection will provide download speeds up to 2Mbps, although in practice, many ISPS are providing much slower rates than this to the first wave of subscribers. ADSL and its variants are already available in the United States and some European countries. Its advance is happening more slowly than anticipated in countries such as the UK, where upgrading telephone exchanges throughout the country is proving to be expensive and time-consuming.

Cable modems connect computers to the Internet via fast cable TV networks. Theoretically capable of much higher speeds than ADSL, cable connections are shared with other local subscribers to the service, reducing performance during busy periods. Cable access is widespread in the United States and Europe, but its availability is more limited than ADSL because of the need to physically install the cables by digging up roads.

Digital satellite networks offer significantly greater download speeds than modem or ISDN-based connections, at around 400Kbps, via a dish that can also receive satellite television. New global satellite systems such as Teledesic will offer cheap, worldwide coverage for those more interested in consuming information than generating it. Because subscribers have no way of transmitting data back to the satellite, all outgoing data (such as a request for a web page) must travel across a standard modem-equipped telephone line.

Digital fibre networks massively increase the amount of information that can be transmitted between computers, allowing speeds of 700Mbps or more. Digital fibre is costly to install and it will be many years before it is widespread, but some cable companies have already introduced such fibre connections in some areas.

In the short term, the choice facing consumers and businesses will be between ADSL and standard coaxial cable. ADSL, regarded by some as wasteful for web browsing but insufficiently powerful for digital media applications such as audio and video, may turn out to be a better bet for businesses. Cable, whose providers are already well established in the entertainment business, appears to be good for consumers interested in video on demand and high-bandwidth video games. They share a subtler but equally important characteristic: continuity. ADSL and cable are both always-on systems, meaning that they maintain permanent connections to the Internet. This has profound implications for the way in which the web is used. Instead of reaching for paper-based atlases or encyclopedias, ADSL or cable subscribers can pull up their web-based equivalents instantly, without the delay or the cost associated with regular dial-up calls. In effect, these connections blur the distinction between a computer and the Internet; the net is just there, in the same way that television or radio is. By upgrading their Internet connections, people are effectively changing their relationship with the vast resource that is the web.

The appliance of science

The way in which we access the Internet is changing not just in terms of the sorts of connections we use, but of the machines we use as well. Currently, nearly everyone who sends e-mail or browses the web does so from a personal computer of one kind or another: a Macintosh or a Windows/Intel box, a notebook or a desktop. Increasingly, though, the pipes that bring us the data we need will feed not into the clumsy, static machines of the late 20th century but into sleek, portable and intelligent information appliances.

Today's PCs are fast and powerful, but they are also error-prone and cumbersome. Attempts to exploit these weaknesses, most notably by Sun Microsystems and its network computer, have so far had little success. To date, PCs have proved to be more useful than any of their proposed alternatives, and so-called thin clients (small, efficient devices relying on streamlined network applications rather than bloated hard disks) have been let down by the failure of the necessary network services to materialise. All this is changing, as small, cheap devices equipped with powerful, low-power processors, abundant memory and wireless facilities communicate with networks based on standard Internet protocols. Although the PC is unlikely to disappear, its importance will inevitably fade as a new way of obtaining and processing information becomes prevalent.

You do not have to look far to see how fast this transition is happening. Catalysed by business and consumer demands for anytime-anywhere communications, the market for wireless net devices is growing at an astonishing speed. A 2000 report from a research company, IDC, predicted that sales of these new information appliances would represent over one-third of the total market for such devices by 2003, with sales exceeding $18 billion in 2004. As the size of the market grows, so does the usefulness of apparently mundane items such as mobile phones, the latest generation of which is equipped with web browsers and e-mail programs as well as the capacity to make plain old phone calls. In 1998 more mobile phones were sold worldwide than cars and PCs combined. In some countries, such as Finland, the number of mobile phone users, and thus the number of potential subscribers to high-speed mobile networks, already exceeds the number of landlines.

The next generation

This growth has generated immense excitement in the high-tech industry, thanks to some new developments in wireless technology. Currently, mobile phones can exchange data with other devices only at miserly speeds that preclude any kind of Internet activity other than the simplest e-mail or text-only web browsing. But over the next three years the bandwidth available to mobile devices will rise dramatically. So-called 3G (third generation) services such as UMTS, due in around 2002, will enable phones, PDAs and any other suitably equipped device to exchange data at up to 2Mbps, nearly 40 times faster than most peoples' current modem connection. Even the intermediate technologies such as GPRS (general packet radio service), expected late in 2000, will boost speeds from their current 9.6Kbps to over twice that of current modems. This will make it possible to have all sorts of new information services at your fingertips.

In conjunction with new developments like WAP (Wireless Application Protocol), mobile phones and PDAS can already be used for banking, share trading, booking theatre tickets or checking sports results. Every major player in the Internet business is planning such services. Microsoft, for example, will provide flight details, travel itineraries and even driving directions from its Expedia travel service; many banks are trying out personal banking services; and information providers such as the BBC are planning to give people on-the-hoof access to their vast websites. In the future, more ambitious applications will be commonplace. You could download the entire contents of a new CD to a music player, for example, in a minute or two, while out jogging or on the bus.

This may sound far-fetched. But many people are determined to make it a reality. The industry buzz has focused on companies developing new wireless technologies, with giants in the field such as Microsoft and phone.com busily acquiring or doing deals with dozens of smaller, often European, newcomers. So frenzied is the interest that the flotation of AT&T's wireless division in April 2000 turned out to be the biggest in American history, raising £10.6 billion on its first day of trading. In the UK, a government auction of high-bandwidth spectrum raised £22.5 billion from just five licences. Wireless spectrum is now deemed so valuable that in New Zealand the Maori community took court action to prevent the government auctioning off a valuable resource that it claimed rights to under the country's founding treaty.

Not everyone has benefited from the wireless revolution. In early 2000, a satellite phone company, Iridium, decommissioned its multibillion-dollar satellite network and went into liquidation, unable to convince a sceptical audience of the need for expensive phone calls from literally anywhere in the world. Making a lasting impact in the online world is a trick that remains independent of the usefulness of the technology – a lesson that many Internet companies around the world are learning the hard way.

THE BUSINESS OF E-BUSINESS

Contrary to what some of the pundits say, the Internet does not change everything. It does change everything that relies on communication, however, and that is quite enough. For businesses, changing the way they communicate means being willing to change the way that companies talk to customers and suppliers, and the way they talk among themselves.

The change in the relationship with customers is the most noticeable. All the people using the Internet know that it can be used to buy things, and quite a lot of them now make use of this. Forrester, an American research company that has come to be treated as an authority in such matters, estimated 1999 retail sales at about $20 billion. It thinks they will rise to $185 billion by 2004, propelled by the increasing range of goods and services on offer, the increasing proportion of Internet users willing to buy online and the absolute increase in the number of people using the Internet. Anyone who has bought bargain books from Amazon or holidays from lastminute.com, or who has found something for sale on the web that they have been unable to find in their high street stores, local shopping mall or even their whole country can understand this optimism. Once you have appreciated the appeal of this sort of shopping, and when you realise how many other people could appreciate it but have not yet done so, such predictions of growth seem unexceptional.

B2B, or not B2B?

Retail e-commerce is highly visible because it has to advertise. But business-to-business (B2B) e-commerce outstrips it in almost every other respect. Estimates of the amount of money being spent by consumers on retail online vary widely, but nobody doubts that the total is dwarfed by B2B transactions. Forrester estimates the value of B2B e-commerce at $1.5 trillion or more by 2003; Gartner Group, another research company, puts it as high as $7.3 trillion by 2004. Although there is little consensus on how you measure these things, one fact about B2B e-commerce is generally recognised: the cost of processing and fulfilling transactions on the Internet is a small fraction of their equivalent in the real world. Systems and people become more productive because these processes are not only cheaper but also much more efficient, taking full advantage of the economies of scale and processing power that the Internet provides.

Technology companies have been quick to exploit both sides of e-commerce, if only because the nature of their business makes them aware of the potential. Dell, a computer manufacturer with revenue of $27 billion in 1999, did nearly half of its business on the web, and Cisco, a company selling the machines that direct the Internet's traffic, sold about 80% of its routers and other devices online in 1998–99. All of Cisco's ordering, fulfilment and payments systems are automated, which the company believes saves it an estimated $500m a year. But you do not have to be Dell or Cisco to benefit from this kind of approach. Companies of all sizes are now looking to the business auction and exchange mechanisms that are blossoming on the web to buy and sell everything from auto parts to almonds, massively reducing their costs and finding business partners that would otherwise have been hard to track down.

There are no rules – except …

Internet companies are astonishingly diverse, and there is little consistency in the way they do business. Nonetheless, there are still some truths that account for its explosive growth into every kind of commerce.

Information is everything. If you sell information in any form at all the Internet matters, and even if you sell something else, information is a critical part of the deal. Retailers that describe and illustrate products (and maybe even provide free samples, as some music websites do) will prosper where others fail; similarly, those that provide accurate delivery times and shipping information will do business where others cannot. This is true of all businesses, because all information is equal on the Internet. CD-quality music, sales data, software, telephone calls, parts catalogues, CVs and photographs are all treated with equanimity.

Geography is dead. Because the Internet is a truly global system, the exact locations of organisations are becoming increasingly irrelevant, at least in some respects. In the retail world, sellers can open up new markets in previously unthought-of places at virtually no cost. Companies can exchange valuable information with each other across borders and time zones with smallish investments in standard Internet technologies. A corollary of this is that time is dying too; whatever time it is, someone who can do what you want is probably awake somewhere in the world. An exception to geography's general demise is that although being physically close to suppliers and customers may matter less, being close to the rest of your business community – the people you gossip with, hire, compete against, and so on – seems to matter as much as ever. If someone from Silicon Valley tells you geography is dead, ask him how much he paid for his house.

The buyer is king. On the Internet another vendor is just one mouse click away, which nullifies a lot of the home-turf advantage sellers have had over buyers. There are always other sources of goods, and there are always other sources of information, including disinterested ones. In particular, customers' ability to compare prices instantly across multiple suppliers is proving to be a powerful price-deflation mechanism.

Keep it simple, stupid

It is one thing to accept these truths. Exploiting them is another matter, and the success or failure of Internet ventures is at least as dependent on strategy as on the technology itself. It requires insight and investment. Electronic shops may not need expensive warehouses or enticing locations (although many of them are investing in these), but they still have their costs. According to a 1999 report by the Gartner Group, an average e-commerce site costs $1m and takes five months to build. Most of the successful Internet companies have spent many times this on their sites, although this does not mean that you have to. It may no longer be true that a website removes all distinctions between large and small companies (as the old joke has it, "on the Internet, nobody knows you're a dog") but it may not matter. Simple websites describing services in a useful way to potential customers and providing relevant contact or booking facilities (much-maligned as "brochureware" by web gurus) may still be enough to boost sales by 15–20%. The key is not to be flash but to be found. A recent British trend, already being followed in the rest of Europe and the United States, may help fix this problem. Small business portals run by companies like BT and VirginNet offer not only advice on building sites but also technical assistance, registering sites with search engines and even providing merchant numbers for trading online at a fraction of the cost of a big web consultancy.

Insight, however, is the crucial ingredient. This means insight not just into the nuts and bolts of the business, but also into the relationships that sustain it. The question is not "What do we sell?" but "How do we find and keep customers?". This is turning out to be harder to answer than anyone expected. Finding people is easy enough, and most Internet companies eventually turn to the marketing and advertising strategies that have sustained old-world businesses for years. Persuading them to drop into your site, however, is harder, as people tire of unexpected e-mail promotions and unimaginative web advertisements. Currently, fewer than one in 200 people click on any given web banner advert in the United States.

We're just trying to keep the customer satisfied

Hardest of all, though, is keeping customers, a trick that only a small number of companies manage with any degree of success. The key to this seems to be good old-fashioned service – an obvious place to start looking, you might think, but one that has proved curiously elusive for most Internet companies. The paragon of Internet company service is still Amazon.com, which manages to deliver its products quickly, efficiently, securely and with the minimum amount of hassle to a customer base with plenty of options to go elsewhere. Amazon is not the cheapest bookstore on the web, nor was it the first, but it retains its lead because it seems to know what its customers want and how to deliver it. Similarly, business is booming for many catalogue-based mail-order companies (which have been keeping their customers satisfied in the real world for years) that have moved their business to the web.

A survey published in early 2000 into the responsiveness of British e-commerce sites should give online retailers pause for thought. Hewson Consulting found that adult entertainment sites were better at replying to urgent requests for information quickly and appropriately than any other kind of retailer, topping the charts in all the categories measured. Proof that these kinds of details matter comes from Datamonitor, a research company, which estimates that 237m online transactions were attempted in 1998 but only 80m of them were completed, because of obstructive or confusing design or a lack of information about the products or services they were selling. It thinks that 8% of the abandoned sales, representing $1.6 billion, could have been saved by implementing some form of online customer service – e-mail or web callback support, for example.

These lessons, and others like them, seem simple. But taking them on board is something else. As some recent and much-publicised failures of Internet companies demonstrate, there is more to building a successful business than merely having lots of money or a big brand behind you. In retail e-commerce, the companies that have got it right have, so far, been those that have paid attention to the small details as well as the more glamorous elements of their business. Those that have failed to do this, such as the clothes and fashion retailer boo.com or the Disney-backed Toysmart, have fallen by the wayside, and many others are sure to join them in the future.

Niche work if you can get it

A more obvious criterion for success in online retailing is selling something that online customers will buy. The web is littered with the 404s of companies that failed to meet this test. In particular, and to the surprise of people who thought that the web was just a new way of publishing things, companies offering access to specific content for sale have done very poorly indeed. There is a lot of information on the web, and people have to want the information on your site a great deal before they will be willing to pay for it. If you offer highly relevant financial advice or particularly appealing pornography you can make a go of this. If you are trying to be a general interest magazine, like Microsoft's *Slate*, or a more widespread information source, like Time Warner's now-extinct *Pathfinder*, experience to date suggests that you cannot. The web offers so much information for free, on such a bewildering variety of subjects and from such an unmatchable range of sources, that people are reluctant to pay for more, no matter how good it is. Instead of selling content to customers, you have to sell consumers' eyeballs to advertisers.

It is interesting to note that a June 2000 survey of popular websites by Nielsen Netratings, a web ratings company, only five of the top 20 were actually selling anything. Most of the other 15 were relying on advertising. Advertising is not the most stable revenue source, but it can be a way of making content pay, and also of making signposts to content pay. This is the business model of the portals, sites that guide surfers to other sites while showing them advertisements for things they might like. For some of these, such as Yahoo, the just-pointing-at-things strategy has been highly successful. Others have failed to get the brand recognition needed to make such a strategy work, especially those with national or global sites with little stratification of users into easily targetable groups. Increasingly, such sites try to show their users not just general information, but information that will be of interest to that specific customer, thus increasing both the likelihood of customer satisfaction and the value of that customer's eyeballs to advertisers interested in those particular tastes.

As Amazon and Yahoo have shown, it is possible to build a brand online. It is also possible to import one wholesale, or simply to buy one. People are bidding furiously to buy promising sounding domain names (such as business.com, which was sold for $7.5 million in February 2000) in the hope that they can turn it into the basis of a profitable business. But the fact that it is possible has not yet made it easy or common. Companies from what might be called the real world have made comparatively few waves on the Internet with their retail businesses, although many are using it for B2B transactions. In 1999 IBM, for example, one of the oldest of old-school technology companies, earned more from its e-business sales alone (about one-quarter of its total) than the top 25 Internet companies managed between them.

In with the old guard?
This state of affairs may be about to change. Established bricks-and-mortar companies have various advantages that mean they could soon invade the Internet. One of these is cash. In itself it is no guarantee of success. Toys 'R' Us, for example, which is highly profitable when selling things in warehouses, struggled to build a successful business when selling things online, even though rivals such as eToys thrive there. But cash certainly helps. So does being able to absorb losses, being immune to overblown stockmarket valuations, having brands that are already household names and being able to drive web business from the starting position of a large customer base. These companies have disadvantages too – a conservative unwillingness to see that to profit on the Internet they will have to undermine some of their

current markets is one of them. They have outlooks shaped in an earlier age. Outlooks can change, however; and some old-fashioned ideas, such as the importance of selling things for more than it cost you to produce or procure them, may yet prove to have value in the online world.

Some commentators have speculated that once the old school gets its act together there will be no "traditional" Internet companies left. Many will be bought. Others will simply wilt under pressure. The rest will adapt and survive in niches and service networks surrounding the biggest fish, whether these fish were spawned online or offline. Whatever happens, it is clear that the move from the offline world to the online one has started. According to analysts at investment bank Hambrecht and Quist, existing companies are gearing up to spend $50 billion or so on Internet services and consultancy in 2000–04. They are hoping to make a smooth transition from their bricks-and-mortar incarnation to the so-called clicks-and-mortar strategy that they trust will keep their businesses alive and competitive in the future.

Details, details

Nearly 40 years after the Internet came into being, and a decade after Tim Berners-Lee and his colleagues conceived the World Wide Web, there is only one real certainty as far the business world is concerned. Nobody knows what a genuinely successful Internet business model looks like, not even those rare companies with real customers and healthy revenue streams. This lies behind much of the global uncertainty over Internet stocks, making institutional investors more cautious about technology stocks and start-up capital harder to find. Meanwhile, companies such as Amazon are becoming possessive about their best ideas, aware that the edge over their competitors might hinge on something as simple as a one-click method of buying goods. Such innovative details could mean the difference between success and failure for Internet companies – an unsettling thought for anyone putting millions into their web business.

THE PLAYERS

In time the Internet will come to matter to every business, in the same way as the telephone does today only more so. But to some companies it is already crucial to their existence. These are the companies that actually create it, and as a result have found themselves caught up in an unprecedented growth business, in which some of them never expected to be involved at all and which could spell the end of even the mightiest.

Take Microsoft. In the early 1990s it was almost inconceivable that Microsoft's position at the top of the technology tree could be under threat. In 1995 and 1996 the company was at the height of its powers. Windows 95 was a huge success. Its traditional competitors – IBM and Apple in operating systems, Lotus and WordPerfect in applications – seemed dead in the water. But already the Internet's power to turn things on their heads was becoming apparent.

Two things happened, one widely noticed at the time and one that became apparent a little later. The first was that Microsoft tripped over the power of the Internet. The company's much ballyhooed online service turned out to be much less popular than it had expected, and surfing the Internet was much more popular than it had expected. What is more, surfing used a type of software – a browser – that Microsoft had never built before. Having stumbled, though, the giant recovered with vigour. Microsoft redefined itself as an Internet company, and threw its considerable weight as a monopolistic seller of PC operating systems at the problem of cracking the Internet market. This about-face was widely applauded at the time, although its legal fallout now darkens the company's future.

Despite Judge Thomas Jackson Penfield's ruling in June 2000 that Microsoft's monopolistic and anti-competitive behaviour should be punished by the breaking-up of the company into an Internet company and an everything-else company, its influence on the Internet is unlikely to fade soon. Despite the self-interested predictions of Java enthusiasts, network-computer proponents, Macintosh evangelists and everyone else who believes that Windows represents an intolerable and eternal constraint on human liberty, it remains the most accessible software of its kind for the millions of people who need to use personal computers. Even if the appeals process fails to reverse Jackson's decision – an outcome which might still be many years hence – there will still be a company making Windows, albeit one with its wings severely clipped. Microsoft's future as an Internet software company is less certain. Forced to compete on level ground with other developers of Internet software, many of which are much better at it than Microsoft, companies like Netscape may once again be able to innovate and even dominate with something like their early vigour.

A subtler but equally profound change is happening in the ecology of software development. Before the Internet, thousands of companies large and small were encouraged by Microsoft to write software that worked with the Windows operating system. This made Windows useful to millions of people and helped Microsoft to see off its competitors. But writing Windows software was hard work, and the prospect of freedom from its unforgiving nature was attractive to many developers. On the web, anyone can write functional software without any programming tools whatsoever. Indeed, the simplest text editor is all that is needed to create big, powerful sites that can be accessed by anyone with an Internet account and a browser. Add some bells and whistles using Sun's Javascript language and you suddenly have commercial applications that can run on any computer, without any need for a Microsoft operating system. There are now many other more interesting things for software developers to play with than Windows, especially as the boundaries between computers and things like phones and PDAs blur, and this will cause a fundamental shift in the technology landscape.

Another big shift is the open-source movement, in which software is developed not as part of a secret proprietary process but in the open. New ideas are tested and peer reviewed by a wide-ranging community, and end up being owned by everybody. Much to the surprise of people who do not have experience of how hackers think, this turns out to be a rather good way of doing things, and the ease of collaboration over the Internet has made it even better. It can also lead to commercial success. In many areas open-source products compete successfully with those designed by big companies.

By far the best-known open-source success is Linux. This is an operating system – a piece of software that turns a dumb pile of chips, cables and disk drives into a computer that can actually do things – that is completely free to anyone who is prepared to download it. With Linux and the right computer you have quite enough power to run an ISP, or a big website. Like its older relative Unix, Linux is being widely used for both of these things. Several companies now make programs that run happily under Linux, with many more under development. Organisations like Red Hat, which packages the software in ways that can be easily used by companies and end-users, are thriving. Such is the interest in the Linux world that VA Linux, a company selling computers and services based on the software, recorded the single biggest first-day rise in value – over 700% – on the day it went public, although its value has since declined significantly.

The meaning of the web

Other changes are afoot, many of which question what it actually means to be an Internet company in the 21st century. In the first few days of 2000, AOL announced a $150 billion takeover of media giant Time Warner, which will create the biggest media business on the planet. This new company will provide not just Internet access, online shopping and information services to dial-up subscribers, but also a vast range of entertainment and some powerful new brands. This many-headed monster, invigorated by the broadband and satellite services the company acquired in the late 1990s, has already caused alarm in the Internet community. Worried that their reach is too limited to compete with such a powerful entity, the world's Internet, media and telecommunications companies are busily looking around for new ways to expand their businesses and retain a stake in the exploding electronic economy.

In particular, the telephone companies that control access to the Internet are gearing themselves up for major changes, especially in the emerging wireless markets that will allow people to access the web on any conceivable kind of portable device. The potential of these markets for mobile commerce (m-commerce), and the opportunity for telcos to create and define new high-volume portals for access to the net, has led to frenzied bidding for licences to operate broadband wireless services all over the world as governments auction off bandwidth that was once thought to be more or less unusable. Around this excitement float companies like Nokia, once merely a high-tech manufacturer of all kinds of electronic equipment but now rapidly becoming an unstoppable brand in its own right, thanks to its powerful branding as the most accessible supplier of phones and other communications devices. There is plenty of room for expansion in the wired world too, as developing countries begin to gain access to the technology that the rest of us take for granted. This is one of the reasons that Lycos, one of the web's earliest players, merged with Spanish telco Terra Networks in mid-2000, with its eye on the vast potential of the Latin American market.

Amid all this new activity, many old stagers continue to do good business despite the fierce competition. Yahoo, Excite, Lycos and AltaVista are still among the top ten most visited sites on the web. Sun Microsystems, a long-time player, has made a lot of noise and won a lot of friends with Java, a tool that brings users freedom from

Windows by letting software programs run on any machine, with any operating system. Real Networks invented a new way of bringing life to websites with its streaming media products, and is still finding new ways of squeezing audio and video into impossibly small pipes. Oracle found new life in an old market, selling big databases to the companies whose websites were dealing with huge amounts of data. On the Internet, everything is up for grabs again.

Part 2

A–Z

A

@

The symbol in E-MAIL addresses that separates the user's name from the DOMAIN NAME. Credit for its first use goes to Ray Tomlinson, an engineer at ARPANET contractor Bolt, Beranek and Newman. Tomlinson wrote the first e-mail programs for machines connected to Arpanet in 1972, choosing the @ symbol from the few available punctuation marks on his Model 33 Teletype and creating the Internet's most recognisable icon in the process.

ACRONYMS

Programmers and technicians use acronyms or abbreviations to reduce lengthy and complicated terms to manageable proportions. Some, when spelled out, are reasonably self-explanatory, such as GUI (graphical user interface). Others, like CORBA, (common object request broken architecture) are rather harder to visualise and remember. Not all acronyms are technical. In NEWSGROUPS you may come across figures of speech such as IMHO (in my humble opinion) and IYSWIM (if you see what I mean).

Although it would be impossible to provide a complete list in a book such as this, many attempts to do so exist on the web – try YAAS (yet another acronym server).

ACTIVEX

A loosely defined set of standards from MICROSOFT for creating software components. Often misleadingly compared with JAVA, the most visible aspects of ActiveX to Internet users are controls, small pieces of software that extend the capabilities of web BROWSERS such as Microsoft's INTERNET EXPLORER and NETSCAPE'S NAVIGATOR. These controls may perform many functions, such as displaying animations or real-time financial data, and can be written in many languages, including Java.

ActiveX has raised many concerns about security on the web. Unlike most other downloadable chunks of code, ActiveX controls can access nearly all the functions of a WINDOWS-based PC, including those relating to the hardware. This gives them great power and flexibility, but exposes unwary users to potential security hazards. A malicious HACKER can easily write small programs that will shut down a computer without warning or delete the entire content of its hard drive. Java fans and many security consultants cite these problems as good reasons to avoid the use of ActiveX. Microsoft, however, says that the use of a DIGITAL SIGNATURE to identify controls from trusted companies will guarantee user security. Whoever is right, it is evident that more and more people are shunning ActiveX in favour of Java APPLETS and FLASH applications.

ADSL

Asymmetric Digital Subscriber Line, one of several digital technologies designed to increase the BANDWIDTH available over standard copper telephone wires (see also DSL). ADSL's design is based on the assumption that most homes and businesses consume more data than they generate. Accordingly, such a connection may theoretically provide an incoming (or downstream) data speed of up to 8MBPS and an outgoing (or upstream) speed of less than 1Mbps, although in practise ISPS are likely to provide much slower connections than this to keep costs down. Thus ADSL is suitable for one-way applications such as video on demand and software distribution, but much less so for those with two-way needs such as videoconferencing. The actual data transmission speeds possible depend on the quality and integrity of the copper connection and associated equipment, as well as the distance of the user from the exchange.

Because ADSL runs on standard copper wires with a direct one-to-one link to the exchange, rather than across shared cable, it will provide much more consistent performance than most of the alternatives. It requires only a special MODEM and, in some cases, a separate device to split the data and voice channels. ADSL is an attractive alternative to ISDN, not least because of its "always-on" characteristic, providing instant access to the Internet alongside simultaneous voice and fax.

ADVERTISING

The Internet has provided yet another medium through which products, services and brands can be promoted through advertising. To website CONTENT providers, getting money from advertisers is a much more attractive proposition than trying to get it from content users. To a potential advertiser the web has unique attractions. Web audiences can be tracked and carefully targeted, and it is easy to monitor which sites visitors come from, how long they spend at an advertiser's site and where they go next. This is hard to do in the real world.

The figures appear to speak for themselves. The Internet Advertising Bureau reported that Internet advertising revenue more than doubled in 1999, amounting to $4.62 billion, and Datamonitor estimates that it will grow to a staggering $36 billion by 2003. But these figures conceal the ever-increasing caution of advertisers, who are becoming more discriminating about where they advertise and more demanding about the terms on which they do so.

One reason for this caution is the decline in the usefulness of the BANNER, still the principal form of advertising on websites. Whereas pioneering sites such as HOTWIRED (the self-proclaimed inventor of the banner ad in 1994) once claimed CLICKTHROUGH rates of 10% or more, the American average is down to less than 0.4% (fewer than one in 200 visitors) according to some estimates. The European average is roughly 4–5 times higher, at 1.5–2% or so, but the trend continues downwards and people are looking for alternatives to plain banners in an attempt to make their advertising more effective. Recent developments include the EXTRAMERCIAL, a new kind of website advertisement that can display more information and therefore theoretically attract more business, as well as the inclusion of video in more conventional banners.

Nevertheless, the number of IMPRESSIONS registered by the big advertisers is growing fast. According to NetRatings, an American ratings firm, a privacy specialist, TRUSTe, registered over 2 billion impressions a month in the first four months of 2000, and agencies such as DoubleClick, which manage the delivery and display of banners on behalf of advertisers, continue to thrive, delivering several billion ad impressions a month. The sites that attract most advertising are the leading PORTAL sites and SEARCH ENGINES such as AOL, YAHOO and LYCOS. Inevitably, they are also the most expensive places to advertise.

Many companies are turning to other, cheaper devices such as affiliate marketing programmes (in which a supplier of goods or services exchanges a link to its website for a share of any profits accruing from sales generated as a result) and E-MAIL advertising to sell more goods ONLINE. AMAZON's affiliate marketing programme, for example, offers websites that display links to its bookselling pages a share of the profits from any resulting book sales. Smaller businesses have been well served by the rise of networks such as the MICROSOFT-owned LinkExchange, which offers schemes including free exchange of banners between sites as well as various inexpensive ways of advertising on high-profile sites such as Yahoo. Some advertisers now regard WEB RINGS as especially useful and well-targeted places to put their banners.

AGENT
A piece of software designed to find and process information automatically, especially across a NETWORK. Grandiose claims are regularly made for the potential of agents, but these have yet to be substantiated. Programs such as GRAND CENTRAL STATION are currently used mainly for retrieving regularly visited web pages, scouring NEWSGROUPS for articles of interest and automating other, similarly repetitive tasks. Despite its current limitations, agent technology remains a hot topic. As the SEARCH ENGINES struggle to keep up to speed with the ever-expanding web, the vaguest promise of intelligent and individually tailored entities that can deliver precisely targeted information is an enticing one for many investors and developers. One area of interest is shopping, where agents

can help by searching retail sites for the best-priced items.

AIN'T IT COOL NEWS

A film critique website run by Texas-based Harry Knowles, now the Internet's most prominent film pundit. Ain't It Cool News has acquired a fearsome reputation among the big film studios, thanks to its detailed reporting and analysis of film screenings and insider secrets several months before the films themselves are released (or even finished, in many cases). Knowles's site is regarded as a premier source of industry gossip and rumours, often supplanting Hollywood magazines as the information source of choice for filmgoers and professionals alike. His network of spies inside the big studios has given him many exclusives, although his apparent scoop listing the 2000 Oscar winners in advance proved to be highly inaccurate, much to the delight of leading film executives, who made the most of their first opportunity to ridicule him for a change.

ALTAVISTA

One of the first search engines for the WORLD WIDE WEB. AltaVista was born at Digital Equipment Corp (DEC) in 1995, the software developed as a result of an internal obsession with keeping track of old e-mail. It now indexes over 200 gigabytes of web-based data. AltaVista was acquired by Compaq as part of its 1998 takeover of Digital, but was sold to investment group CGMI in 1999 in a deal that valued the company at $2.7 billion.

AltaVista caused a stir in Europe in early 2000 when it announced the launch of a free ISP service, complete with free phone calls, the first time any company had announced intentions to do so. Several other companies have since followed suit, including LYCOS.

AMAZON

Almost certainly the most visible brand born on the web and one of the most talked-about companies in the brief history of the Internet. Amazon was founded by Jeff Bezos in 1994 with the aim of being able to deliver any book in print in the United States, over 1m titles at that time. By June 1999 it had become the first Internet company to reach 10m customers (and in fact gained over 10m new customers in 1999 alone, finishing the year with a total of over 16m). At the same time, *Forbes* magazine rated Bezos's personal worth at over $10 billion and the company was worth twice as much as British Airways.

First Internet company to reach 10m customers: Amazon, June 1999.

Bezos's most important contribution to the Internet economy has been people; more precisely, shoppers prepared to hand over details of their credit cards to a website. No other organisation has done as much to acclimatise people to the idea that buying things on the Internet is safe. So successful has it been in this regard that Amazon now sells not just books but also videos, CDs, toys, games, health and beauty products and even DIY equipment, with pharmaceuticals, groceries and other "referral" products (those it does not need to stock) expected to follow. Amazon's book-selling operations started as a referral-type business with books sourced from wholesalers when they were ordered, but now Amazon is building warehouses to hold its own stock. As if all this was not enough, the company has added an auction service and a scheme for third parties to sell their goods on the Amazon site, called Zshops, and has taken over several high-profile specialist interest sites, including the highly rated Internet Movie Database.

Like most Internet companies, Amazon has achieved all this without ever making a profit. Its share price in the period June 1998–June 1999 ranged from a low of around $22 to a high of $221, and despite a 169% increase in 1999 revenue to $1.64 billion, the company is still losing money – $122m in the first quarter of 2000 alone. Jeff Bezos himself became unpopular among the web community in early 2000, when he patented several features of the Amazon website and took legal action to prevent competitors using their own versions of the 1-Click ordering system.

ANON.PENET.FI

A Finnish computer system used to protect the identities of Internet users (see REMAILER).

AOL

America On Line, the world's largest provider of Internet access and ONLINE SERVICES, with over 22 million subscribers and another 2.7 million under the CompuServe umbrella. AOL made its mark on the world by attracting subscribers with interactive services such as CHAT, via the distribution of hundreds of millions of trial disks – comfortably the biggest such marketing programme in history. It then exchanged access to those subscribers for original CONTENT from big media names such as Time Warner, CBS and New Line Cinema, alongside free ADVERTISING with those companies. The result is a service rich in information, plush with visitors and busily generating real money.

Despite this success story, there can be few Internet companies that attract as much vitriol as AOL – or AOHell, as it is known in some circles. It is often criticised for its poor service to dial-up subscribers, its nannying and censorious behaviour, the ineptitude of its software and a huge SPAM problem. There are several websites and NEWSGROUPS devoted entirely to these issues – aolsucks.org being a representative example.

None of this has slowed CEO Steve Case down for a moment. The company, which has long regarded itself as a media concern as well as a provider of online services, has spent much of the last few years figuring out ways to bring its content to ever more people, in ever more varied ways. Nobody was very surprised when AOL bought NETSCAPE in 1998, marking its first real interest in the business sector. The company spent much of 1999 forging deals with suppliers of BROADBAND and satellite communications in a big push to provide subscribers with high-speed access to its enhanced services. It moved into online music distribution, buying two digital music companies, and it has made some aggressive moves towards the retail sector as a whole; deals were signed with AMAZON.COM, flower sellers and other suppliers of goods online.

The big question facing AOL was how to tie these threads together in a way that maximised its chances of staying at the head of the pack. Its astounding answer came in January 2000, when it announced a $150 billion takeover of entertainment giant Time Warner, creating by far the world's biggest media company in the process. In a deal that gives it access to 100 million subscribers, immense distribution networks, a wide variety of new content resources and some powerful new brands, AOL has once again changed the competitive landscape of the new media business.

APACHE

Software for running web SERVERS. Unlike similar software from giants such as NETSCAPE and MICROSOFT, Apache is free, which has led to its rapid adoption by millions of websites. A Netcraft survey in May 2000 showed that 61% of websites polled were running Apache, putting it streets ahead of commercial products such as Microsoft's IIS (21%) and Netscape's Enterprise Server (5%).

Apache, so named because it was originally based on a "patchy" version of an NCSA web server, runs on many kinds of computers, including Intel-based WINDOWS NT machines and UNIX-based systems, and is an important part of the OPEN SOURCE movement. Not only is the actual program code freely downloadable, but so is the editable SOURCE CODE, making it possible for users to customise the software.

APPLET

A small computer program usually dedicated to a specific task. In the context of the WORLD WIDE WEB, applets are built into web pages to perform functions such as displaying animations or performing calculations. Typically written in JAVA, such programs are designed to run in any BROWSER supporting that language.

ARPANET

A pioneering NETWORK that formed the basis of the Internet. Arpanet began life in 1969 as a testbed for new networking technologies funded by the United States Defense Advanced Research Project Agency (DARPA). Its decentralised structure, in which no single NODE has overall control of the network, was conceived amid concerns about the vulnerability of centralised structures to sudden upsets (such as nuclear war). The networks that replaced Arpanet (a new military network, the Defense Data Network, and NSFNet, a network of scientific and academic computers funded by the United States' National Science Foundation) evolved into the BACKBONE of today's Internet. The process continues as this backbone is turned over to a consortium of commercial providers.

ASP

Active Server Pages, a popular technique for automatically generating web pages from a template held on a SERVER. In conjunction with customised SCRIPTS, ASP extracts appropriate information from a DATABASE and formats it as HTML before sending it to a BROWSER. One of MICROSOFT's rare original inventions for the web, ASP is especially useful for automatically updating corporate information and other pages whose structure rarely changes. Originally designed for WINDOWS NT, ASP has been converted by ChiliSoft for use with a number of UNIX variants. SUN MICROSYSTEMS thought the concept so impressive that it produced a similar technology called JAVA Server Pages.

ASYNCHRONOUS TRANSFER MODE

A networking technology enabling fast transfer of information. Asynchronous transfer mode (ATM) promises extremely high data transfer rates, perhaps up to 10 gigabytes per second, although current implementations are limited to about

600MBPS, roughly six times the speed of the fastest LOCAL AREA NETWORKS in popular use.

ATM is something of a hybrid, borrowing elements of both PACKET-SWITCHING and CIRCUIT-SWITCHING techniques for moving data between two points. ATM hardware splits data into packets of a fixed size, 53 BYTES to be exact, of which 48 bytes constitute data and the remaining 5 bytes routing and priority information. Unlike other packet-switching technologies, however, the system then sends each chunk of data over a predetermined route, rather than routing each along the most convenient available path and reassembling at the destination point.

ATM's proponents, sometimes known as BELL-HEADS, say that ATM's high-speed connections hold the answer to the Internet BANDWIDTH problem They point out that its ability to manage traffic volumes and billing will make life easier for ISPs. It also provides an easy way to organise the priority of one type of data over another, so that data for real-time applications such as videoconferencing can be sent ahead of less time-critical data such as E-MAIL. Internet purists (NETHEADS) say that it is inflexible and potentially dangerous, as a single break in a connection causes that whole connection to collapse. But not everyone working on the net is a total nethead. Some big ISPs are installing ATM equipment, and CISCO Systems, the biggest supplier of IP switches for the Internet, has invested in ATM switch manufacturers.

ATTACHMENT

A file sent with an E-MAIL message, such as a document or an audio clip. Any disk file can be sent as an attachment, although size is often a limitation for those with slow MODEM connections; sending unannounced huge video segments to friends is generally regarded as bad form.

Files sent as attachments from e-mail programs must be converted into a text-based format using a process known as encoding. The text is then converted back into BINARY FILE format at the receiving end. The most common encoding systems for the PC are UUENCODE and MIME; Macintoshes commonly use BINHEX. Such conversions occasionally cause problems, as not all e-mail programs understand all formats; this is why e-mail sometimes arrives as pages of seemingly incomprehensible garbage, rather than the expected document or spreadsheet. A bigger contemporary problem is that of VIRUSES such as Melissa and I Love You, many of which now arrive in the form of e-mail attachments.

ATM

See ASYNCHRONOUS TRANSFER MODE. This is also the abbreviation for Adobe Type Manager, a font-smoothing program used by Macintosh and WINDOWS machines in conjunction with desktop publishing programs and word processors; and for automated teller machine, a device that dispenses cash. Technology has unfortunately outstripped the alphabet's capacity to abbreviate it (see TLA).

AVATAR

A software-generated figure or form taken by a participant in an ONLINE world, gaming environment or CHAT room. Such representations can take many forms, from free-floating heads to cartoon characters. Many avatars have some sort of three-dimensional characteristics, so that fellow participants can move around them. The word comes from the Hindu religion, where it is used to denote a divine incarnation or deity.

B2B

The common abbreviation for BUSINESS-TO-BUSINESS E-COMMERCE. Contrast with B2C.

B2B EXCHANGE

A website where goods and services are exchanged between buyers and sellers, usually focused on a particular industry or area of interest. Almost anything can be bought and sold in a variety of ways on such sites, and they have attracted traders in commodities as diverse as almonds and petrochemicals. Because of the substantially lower costs of trading ONLINE these electronic trading exchanges are growing rapidly in number, according to a report by a research company, Gartner Group. Over 2,500 were expected in the United States at the end of 1999, with as many as 25,000 anticipated by 2001.

Such exchanges have attracted much attention and publicity, but in common with many E-COMMERCE businesses their likely success is hard to predict. To make profits on small percentages of transactions (as little as 0.2% in most cases) sites need to generate huge volumes of business, a problem in the vertical markets in which most exchanges currently operate. Most of the sites doing significant business rely on a small number of customers, with many making as much as 50% of their revenue from just one or two big traders.

B2C

Short for business-to-consumer, a term used to describe the exchange of goods and services between businesses and the buying public. B2C represents the most glamorous and visible face of ONLINE commerce, despite the fact that the value of retail transactions is considerably smaller than that of their business-to-business equivalents – about $20 billion in the United States in 1999, compared with $109 billion for B2B transactions, according to research company Forrester. Confidence in the B2C market suffered in early 2000 after the collapse of several high-profile businesses, including the much-hyped boo.com in Europe, and most high-tech investors are now turning their attention towards the more lucrative corporate opportunities of B2B.

BACKBONE

A high-capacity line carrying enormous amounts of Internet traffic over long distances. Backbones are typically built and funded by large commercial ISPs such as UUNET and BT in the UK and Sprint and MCI in the United States. The present-day Internet evolved from government-funded American backbones such as NSFNET, originally built to connect research and education communities.

Smaller local and regional networks such as those operated by smaller ISPs connect to the big Internet backbones via connection points known as network access points (NAPS). In the UK, the main NAPS are LINX (London Internet Exchange) and MANAP (Manchester Network Access Point). In the United States, the biggest NAPS are the Metropolitan Area Exchanges (MAES). These access points also connect ISPs to international backbones. For example, large ISPs in many countries connect directly to the backbones operated by Concert, the international network service owned by BT and MCI.

BANDWIDTH

A measure of the range of frequencies occupied by a data signal across a communications channel. The greater the range of frequencies, the more data and thus information can be transmitted in a given time. The term is normally used to refer to the actual amount of information a communications connection can carry; its capacity, in effect.

Generally, the bandwidth required for any given purpose is directly related to the complexity of the task. It takes far more bandwidth to download a full-page colour picture in one second, for example, than a page of plain text; a fact that most regular web users now readily appreciate. In analog systems, such as telephone and television, bandwidth is measured in cycles per second, or hertz (Hz). A typical voice signal occupies about 3 kilohertz (kHz), but a broadcast television signal occupies about 6 megahertz (MHz), or 2,000 times as much. In digital systems, bandwidth is measured in bits per second (bps) and multiples thereof; kilobits per second (KBPS), megabits per second (MBPS) and gigabits per second (Gbps).

There is much confusion about exactly what the bandwidth of networks in widespread use really means in terms of performance. For example, 56K modems can transmit information at only half the 56,000bps that the name promises, and 10Mbps Ethernet connections typically achieve only one-third of the advertised speed. Nevertheless, size is everything in the Internet world, and both hardware manufacturers and telcos are well aware of the marketing pull of larger numbers. Increased bandwidth is the key to providing enhanced web offerings, such as video and audio applications (including broadcast-quality television), and large-scale software distribution. With this in mind, the world's communications companies are racing to build networks that can support a rapidly expanding population of sophisticated and demanding consumers of information.

The process of building a communications infrastructure that will support affordable high-speed Internet access is complex and expensive, and bandwidth providers inevitably pass these costs on to their customers. Although many ISPs now provide free (and slow) individual Internet access, anyone determined to avail themselves of the fastest T1 or T3 connections can expect to pay handsomely for the privilege. Nevertheless, the imminent arrival of technologies such as ADSL should encourage bandwidth consumers to abandon their slowcoach modems. A significant forthcoming development is the huge increase in wireless bandwidth as wireless operators introduce new 3G (third-generation) services offering speeds of up to 2MBPS. Only one thing is certain – however fast your connection, CONTENT providers will find a way to use every last BYTE of it.

BANNER

An advertisement on a web page, usually in the form of a GIF IMAGE. Invented by HOTWIRED in 1994, the banner is the most common form of web advertising and still the source of most of its revenue. Most banners contain animations designed to catch a browser's eye and trigger a CLICK-THROUGH to a website with the hope of eliciting a sale. Banners are sold on a cost per thousand model (CPM), with advertisers typically paying between $10 and $100 or so for every 1,000 IMPRESSIONS, depending on the profile of the site and the position of the advertisement within it.

The effectiveness of banners has declined significantly as their presence has spread to every corner of the web and the curiosity of the audience has waned. Most estimates suggest that passers-by now click on fewer than one in 200 banners on American websites. Nonetheless, they are still regarded as effective tools, especially in conjunction with a SEARCH ENGINE capable of displaying specific banners triggered by particular KEYWORDS. A new generation of interactive banners is appearing, often written as JAVA APPLETS, which provide entertainment or information; golf games, for example, or product catalogues.

BBS

See BULLETIN BOARD.

BCC

Short for blind carbon copy, a copy of an E-MAIL sent to a third party without the primary recipient's knowledge (see CC).

BEENZ

An online currency system, used to buy goods and services on hundreds of websites all over the world. A kind of e-air miles scheme. Subscribers to this free service earn their currency, the eponymous beenz, simply by doing things ONLINE, such as visiting websites, registering with online businesses, shopping or simply accessing the web through their ISP. Once earned, beenz can be spent on many different goods and services online, irrespective of geographic location. This neat variation on the micropayments idea has not yet fully captured the attention of either the browsing public or the retailers and businesses at the back end of the chain, although many big names such as Woolworths, Halifax, Excite and MORI are participants. Other similar schemes exist on the web, including MyPoints.

BELLHEAD

Describes an engineer, manager or marketer with a phone company background, especially one that believes in traditionally rigid principles of solving networking problems with dedicated hardware and fixed connections rather than intelligent software. Bellheads are said to be especially prevalent in companies promoting ATM networks, and they are reviled by IP-worshipping NETHEADS. The name comes from the now-defunct Bell telephone company in the United States, the mother of all phone companies.

BINARY FILE

Technically, a file in which all eight BITS of its component BYTES are used for data. Unlike ASCII-format text files, which contain only generic keyboard characters that can be read by any computer, binary files often contain code specific to the sort of processor in the machine that created the file. This is why binary files attached to E-MAIL messages must be converted to seven-bit ASCII before being sent to a recipient who may be using a different machine.

Not all binary files contain processor-specific codes. Graphics files, for example, use all eight bits for data but use no machine code. Other examples of binary files include spreadsheets, programs such as WINDOWS .exe files and word-processor documents.

BINHEX

A utility for converting Macintosh files into text before transmission across a NETWORK or as part of an E-MAIL message (see ATTACHMENT).

BIT

Short for binary digit; in other words, a one or a zero. Bits are the building blocks of Internet data. Every digital transmission consists of a stream of bits travelling between two points, and most descriptions of BANDWIDTH measure it in bits per second (bps). Eight bits make up a byte.

BLOCKING SOFTWARE

Programs that prevent access to parts of the Internet deemed to be objectionable, sometimes called censorware or filtering software. Blocking software can stop people accessing particular websites, NEWSGROUPS, MAILING LISTS and CHAT lines, and can even prevent them from typing names, addresses or offensive words. Originally designed to protect children from online PORNOGRAPHY and other perceived dangers on the Internet, many commercial blocking products exist and are now in widespread use in the corporate world. Some BROWSERS, for example, MICROSOFT'S INTERNET EXPLORER, contain facilities for controlling access to websites that have been rated by the RSAC scheme.

Blocking software has been heavily criticised for mindlessly discriminating against many harmless sites. Some products, for example, have blocked access to any site or newsgroup containing the word "breast" irrespective of its nature, preventing access by anyone seeking advice on breast cancer. Outraged by this idiocy, two HACKERS reverse-engineered the CyberPatrol blocking software package in 1999 and distributed a program allowing people to see the list of sites being blocked. Mattel, the program's owners, responded with a lawsuit that forced Matthew Skall and Eddy Jansson to hand over the program and refrain from distributing further copies. No one was surprised when it also released a new version of the software that blocked all the sites that had distributed their hack.

BLOWFISH

A strong ENCRYPTION algorithm written by Bruce Schneier in 1993. Blowfish is based on a symmetric

PRIVATE KEY method, taking a key of between 32 and 448 BITS. It is fast, free and above all unbroken, making it suitable for many commercial applications and a useful alternative to DES.

BLUETOOTH

A set of specifications for wireless communications. Bluetooth, named after a king who united Danish provinces in the 10th century, connects electronic devices such as mobile PCS and telephones together across radio waves. Originally started by mobile phone makers Ericsson and Nokia, the Bluetooth consortium is now backed by industry giants such as Intel, IBM and Toshiba and over 1,000 other members.

Bluetooth-compliant devices can communicate with each other within a range of 10m or so (or up to 100m if signals are boosted by a powerful transmitter). In the short term, the biggest promise of this technology is that it will free users from the need to carry cumbersome proprietary cables around. Instead, devices need merely be within range of each other's radio signals to communicate. It is also an excellent way to provide universal data access from single access points; for example, enabling public access to the Internet in railway stations or airports. The first Bluetooth-compliant devices started to arrive early in 2000.

BOOKMARK

A link to a website address, kept by a BROWSER as part of a list of favourite sites. Nearly all browsers use this term; an exception is MICROSOFT'S INTERNET EXPLORER, which refers to such links as favorites. Bookmarks are notoriously clumsy to manage, as most web users amass a huge list of sites. Modern browsers now include features that remember recent or often-visited sites and help users return to them quickly.

BROADBAND

Strictly, a form of data transmission in which several parallel channels pass across a single cable or wire. A good example of a true broadband medium is cable TV, which pumps huge amounts of data to viewers across very fast landlines. The term is used more generically to describe high-speed circuits and signals, especially those relating to fast-growing Internet technologies such as ADSL and cable. Many CONTENT providers and PORTALS are upgrading their systems in preparation for the rapid uptake of broadband by consumers, and are preparing to offer enhanced high-BANDWIDTH services based on audio and video.

Few influential people involved with the Internet claim that it is a good in and of itself. It is a powerful tool for solving social problems, just as it is a tool for making money, finding lost relatives, receiving medical advice, or, come to that, trading instructions for making bombs.
Esther Dyson, *New Perspective Quarterly*, spring 1997

BROWSER

Software for viewing web pages, and thus the key to the explosion of the Internet in the 1990s. Browsers have come a long way since their text-only beginnings at CERN in the early 1990s. Kick-started in 1993 by the NCSA's MOSAIC, the browser business was transformed by NETSCAPE in 1994, with MICROSOFT belatedly joining the party in late 1996. The latest versions of programs such as Microsoft's INTERNET EXPLORER, Netscape's NAVIGATOR and Opera Software's OPERA are more than just HTML viewers; they are sophisticated MULTIMEDIA tools in their own right. Modern browsers can play high-quality audio and video; manage secure connections to E-COMMERCE sites; send and receive E-MAIL; and run JAVA APPLETS, ACTIVEX controls and PLUG-INS that extend their capabilities in other ways.

It is their status as doorways to the web, however, which has made browsers the subject of fierce debate in the net COMMUNITY, a source of acrimony among software vendors and, ultimately, the cause of the highest-profile anti-trust case in recent American history. Own the browser, the theory goes, and you own the web audience and maybe its wallet too – a theory to which Netscape and Microsoft have readily subscribed. Netscape's seemingly unassailable market share of over 80% in 1996 had been steadily whittled away by Microsoft to less than 25% at the beginning of 2000, largely because of the latter's inclusion of its browser software with the latest version of the WINDOWS OPERATING SYSTEM, an act that led to a high-profile antitrust suit against the company. Along the way, both sides have conducted dirty-tricks campaigns, introducing their own extensions to the standards on which the web is based in an effort to seduce developers and users with new and exotic features.

The so-called browser wars have imposed various costs on web users and on site builders, whose lives have been made especially difficult by the need to build support for multiple versions of several different browsers into their code. Many choose to favour one product over another, hence the profusion of "This site is best viewed with ..." notices on websites. However, increasing numbers of users and developers have been favouring Internet Explorer, owing to its wider availability and delays to new versions of Navigator. Whether Netscape can ever regain its lost ground depends on the eventual fate of Microsoft's browser. In the light of Judge Thomas Penfield Jackson's decision that the company illegally and unfairly prevented its rivals from competing in the browser market, it could be forced to remove its browser from the Windows package altogether, an outcome that would allow Netscape to compete on level terms again. Without the immense distribution mechanism that Windows offers, Internet Explorer is just another piece of free software; a painful truth that Microsoft may yet have to face.

BULLETIN BOARD

A computer system used for posting electronic messages, storing files and chatting with other users. Many bulletin board systems (BBS) are devoted to particular topics; others serve the interests of a variety of special interest and discussion groups. Anyone with a computer and a MODEM can start a bulletin board providing they have the right software. This led to the establishment of over 50,000 such systems worldwide by the beginning of the 1990s.

Despite a strong and distinctive culture, the popularity of bulletin boards has declined with the growth of the Internet, largely because many of their functions can be easily duplicated on websites that are reachable by any Internet user instead of only a handful of individuals. However, many bulletin board systems now operate their own websites alongside their original BBS software and remain prosperous.

BURN RATE

The rate at which a new company or venture spends its capital while waiting for profitability. Most Internet START-UP companies are well acquainted with this term, which is widely used in an industry where money is routinely spent much faster than it is earned.

BUSINESS-TO-BUSINESS

Describes the exchange of goods, services, information or money between businesses. Although most of the attention in the E-COMMERCE world has so far been focused on consumer and retailing ventures, most analysts predict that the biggest money will be spent (and earned) in the business sector, with retail accounting for only 10% or so of the total Internet economy. The Gartner Group, a research company, estimates that the total size of the business-to-business (B2B) market may be as much as $7.3 trillion by 2004, although research companies differ widely on how to measure it accurately.

For many companies, it is the savings in time and money that make the B2B sector so appealing. By adopting Internet technology, they can procure goods more cheaply, process invoices more efficiently and deal with customers more effectively. A 1999 report by the Giga Information

Group estimated that doing business ONLINE will save companies around the world an estimated $1.25 trillion by 2002, and other studies show that average delivery times for goods and services may be reduced by up to 95%.

BYTE
Eight bits (see BIT).

BYTECODE
The constituent code in a JAVA program file (see VIRTUAL MACHINE).

C++

An OBJECT-ORIENTED programming language. Bjarne Stroustrop created C++ at Bell Labs in the 1980s as the successor to C, the most popular language for writing software for PCs. C++ is widely regarded as the best language for large-scale projects and applications, although much of its thunder has been stolen by JAVA, another object-oriented language, which many say is easier and more elegant to use.

> *The most important thing in the programming language is the name. A language will not succeed without a good name. I have recently invented a very good name and now I am looking for a suitable language.*
> Donald Knuth

CABLE MODEM

A MODEM enabling the connection of a PC to a local cable television line. Cable modems provide fast, always-on connections to the Internet in areas where the necessary coaxial cable has been laid. They can theoretically achieve data-transfer speeds of up to 30MBPS, but in practice they are limited by the speed of an ISP's Internet GATEWAY. Most European systems provide a data-transfer rate closer to 1.5Mbps, still much faster than prevalent modems or ISDN lines, although this BANDWIDTH is shared between all local users of the cable.

CACHE

An area on a computer's hard disk used by a web BROWSER to store recently downloaded pages. When a user returns to a stored page, it is retrieved from the cache rather than the original Internet SERVER, loading the page faster and reducing the load on the NETWORK. Some ISPs cache popular sites on their own servers, allowing users to DOWNLOAD a local copy rather than the original from a busy remote site.

Other types of cache include a disk cache, used by an OPERATING SYSTEM as a temporary store for the most recently accessed data and program code; and a memory cache, where a computer's processor stores what it thinks will be the next set of instructions it needs from a running program.

CC

A copy of an E-MAIL message sent to one or more recipients other than the main addressee. The other recipients' addresses appear in the cc box at the top of the message so the principal recipient can see who else it was sent to. Most e-mail programs also include a blind carbon copy (BCC) function, which copies the message invisibly; that is, addresses in the BCC box will not be seen by other recipients. The term dates back to a time when the only way of creating a copy of a letter or memo typed on a typewriter was to lay a sheet of carbon paper between two sheets of typing paper, thus creating a carbon impression of the original on the lower sheet.

CDA

Communications Decency Act, part of the Telecommunications Act signed by Bill Clinton in 1996 but overturned by the courts in 1997. Regarded by opposition groups as a violation of the First Amendment, the CDA was criticised for the vagueness of definition of some key terms and its potential use as a means for the government to prosecute over any online activity of which it disapproved (see CENSORSHIP).

CDMA

Code Division Multiple Access, a wireless telephone transmission technology that spreads digitised data across the entire BANDWIDTH of a channel. CDMA technology differs greatly from that of the GSM service widespread in Europe, although it is compatible with the PCS (Personal Communications Services) standard found in the United States. Several large American telcos have announced plans to adopt CDMA as their wireless transmission standard.

C

CENSORSHIP

The growth of the Internet has highlighted issues of censorship, that is the banning of material considered to be against the public interest. Child PORNOGRAPHY, terrorism and other crimes have kept the censorship issue on the agenda of many governments, despite its inherent problems.

Part of the problem is the easy global reach of the Internet. Laws on such matters as indecency and obscenity vary widely from country to country. What is acceptable in Italy may not be in Iran. Even within national boundaries debate persists over what sorts of CONTENT should be regulated. In the United States one answer was the Communications Decency Act (CDA), signed by Bill Clinton in 1996 but overturned by the courts the following year. Their ruling that regulation of speech on the Internet was unconstitutional followed months of challenges from civil liberties groups, ISPS, content providers and Internet enthusiasts.

Some countries have denied access to particular sites at ISP level or blocked specific addresses on individual PCS. The first approach has been tried several times. Most notably, in 1995 the Bavarian authorities in Germany forced CompuServe to close down over 200 NEWSGROUPS, but the company reinstated the groups days later after worldwide complaints. Other attempts to prevent citizens accessing undesirable material, such as criticisms of government policy in Singapore or neo-Nazi sites in the United States, have resulted in material moving rapidly from SERVER to server and becoming more rather than less widely available.

BLOCKING SOFTWARE, often used to protect children from exposure to undesirable material, regularly falls down for two reasons. First, there is a significant problem of scale. Anyone who would censor pornography unilaterally, for example, must attempt to restrict access to many thousands of websites and newsgroups in dozens of countries – a task not so much daunting as impossible, even for companies specialising in filtering so-called bad content from good. Second, most such software must be configured and administered by parents, who are usually no match for their ten-year-old children when it comes to technology.

The last hope for censors is self-regulation by websites and ONLINE SERVICE providers (OSPS). Attempts by OSPS to censor material themselves have led to several embarrassments. AOL, in particular, faced savage criticism when its screening software accidentally shut down a forum for discussing breast cancer because it mentioned breasts. Other content providers have met more success with RSAC, a ratings scheme administered by the Recreational Software Advisory Council in Washington, DC. RSAC's success will depend on two highly unpredictable variables: the correct configuration of web BROWSERS by parents or administrators, and the willingness of website owners to rate their sites accurately, honestly or indeed at all. To date, it is far from accepted practice to do so.

> *The net interprets censorship as damage, and routes around it.*
> John Gilmore

CENSORWARE
See BLOCKING SOFTWARE.

CERN
The European Laboratory for Particle Physics, CERN (formerly the Conseil Européen pour la Recherche Nucléaire, hence the acronym) is famed as the origin of the WORLD WIDE WEB. An initiative to improve collaboration among workers in the physics community, led by Tim Berners-Lee and Robert Cailliau, led directly to the development of HTML, HTTP, the first text-only BROWSER and the first web SERVER. The rest is history.

CERTIFICATE
See DIGITAL SIGNATURE.

C

CGI
Common Gateway Interface, a PROTOCOL that helps to extend the capabilities of otherwise dumb web pages. CGI links a web page to a small computer program that performs a specific task, such as processing the contents of a form and sending back a confirmation message. A CGI program, known as a SCRIPT, can be written in several languages, including PERL, C++ and JAVA. Many web developers now use ASP in preference to CGI.

CHAT
One of the most popular uses of the Internet, particularly among newcomers, and widely regarded as the driving force behind the success of AOL. Once viewed as merely a net enthusiast's version of CB radio, chat is now seen as a critical part of ONLINE COMMUNITY-building and is attracting the attention of most of the big players in the Internet world. A good illustration of chat's success is the program ICQ (bought by AOL in 1998), which has over 50m registered users.

Chat on the Internet takes many forms, from the free-for-all Internet Relay Chat (IRC) channels to one-to-one programs such as ICQ and AOL's Instant Messenger. Most work around a simple, text-only window where messages to an individual or group are typed and the responses read. Many people use chat as a cheap alternative to long-distance or international phone calls, but channels and rooms on many thousands of subjects exist, and some services allow users to set up their own private rooms for more intimate conversations.

Sex is probably the biggest draw in the chat world, either in carefully moderated teenage flirting forums or in rather more forthright private rooms or IRC channels. Whatever the subject of conversation, it has one priceless attribute for the commercially minded: it holds the attention of visitors and keeps them on site. This makes chat a potentially lucrative application for advertisers, who can target specific rooms. With this in mind, no doubt, SEARCH ENGINES such as Excite now include chat features.

A late entrant to the chat world was MICROSOFT, which submitted a proposal to the IETF in 1997 for a new, open and standardised chat PROTOCOL called Rendezvous. This as yet unratified scheme was hatched with the aim of wrestling people away from proprietary software and into a vendor-independent – or, at least, AOL-independent – mainstream. The company's long-awaited MSN Messenger appeared in the summer of 1999, and caused immediate controversy by allowing its users to connect to AOL's chat software. AOL immediately blocked access from the Microsoft product, whereupon Microsoft tweaked Messenger to by-pass the block. This first "chat war" ended in stalemate shortly afterwards, but it rekindled interest in proposals for an open chat standard. Meanwhile, proprietary systems continue to thrive.

CHURN
The rate at which customers abandon subscriptions to a service, usually in favour of a competitor. Churn is an unfortunate fact of life in the ISP business. Consumers, especially those with portable E-MAIL addresses, show a distressing tendency to defect when offered a better option. Rates of 3–4% per month are not unusual, causing headaches for marketing departments already hard-pressed to attract new customers.

CIRCUIT-SWITCHED
Describes a NETWORK in which the two ends of a connection are linked by a fixed circuit. For the duration of this connection the communicating parties have exclusive use of the BANDWIDTH it provides. Ordinary telephone voice calls are circuit-switched. Contrast with PACKET-SWITCHED.

CISCO
The company that connects up the majority of the world's networks. The California company, with revenue now measured in billions of dollars, started life at STANFORD UNIVERSITY, where Sandy Lerner and Len Bosack worked out a way to connect up the computer systems in different build-

ings on campus. Cisco now controls over two-thirds of the world ROUTER market. In 1990 Lerner and Bosack famously sold their two-thirds stake in the company for around $170m; in August 1999 that stake would have been worth over $5 billion.

CLICK

One of the defining activities of the WORLD WIDE WEB. Mouse clicks take visitors from one web page or site to another by way of the HYPERLINKS on which the web is based. Much to the delight of advertisers, they also take people from a suitably attractive BANNER to a place where they can be sold things.

In five years, there won't be any Internet companies because they'll all be Internet companies. Otherwise they will die.
Andy Grove

CLICKS AND MORTAR

Describes a company with its roots and assets in the old economy that also exploits the power of the Internet to expand and streamline its business. A good example is Barnes and Noble, a traditional bookseller that was forced to embrace the web following the success of AMAZON.

Although some observers feel that "pure-play" Internet companies still outperform their slower-moving real-world competitors in many areas, evidence is growing that these new hybrids have some significant advantages. A report by the Boston Consulting Group showed that in 1999 clicks-and-mortar companies acquired customers more cheaply (at an average of $12 each) than net companies (at an average of $82 each). Better-established brands and a lesser need to spend money on offline ADVERTISING mean that offline companies' overall marketing spend is much lower – 36% of revenue, compared with a business-crippling 119% for net purists. However, Internet specialists often retain an advantage in order fulfilment, thanks to the efficiencies of their specially built systems.

CLICKSTREAM

A record of the clicks made as web users travel within and between sites, and thus a record of the pages visited and the order in which they were visited. Web marketers and advertisers use clickstream information to determine the popularity of site sections, time spent on various activities, usability of individual features and the response to BANNER advertisements.

CLICKTHROUGH

An advertising term for a single instance of a CLICK on an advertisement. Clickthroughs are regarded as a better way of measuring and paying for audience response than the number of IMPRESSIONS, as they imply real interest on the part of the viewer. However, clickthrough rates have declined dramatically as web audiences tire of BANNERS, and many advertisers have been forced to pay for the number of times a banner is displayed, irrespective of whether or not somebody clicks on it.

CLIENT/SERVER

Describes a computing model in which one program, a client, requests information from another, a SERVER. The client/server model is one of the most important concepts in NETWORK computing, as it provides a good way for organisations to make use of programs and data that are distributed widely across different machines or networks. Client programs residing on an single PC, for example, might access specific data files such as graphics or documents from a local FILE SERVER, but obtain sales information from a DATABASE in a different country. The WORLD WIDE WEB is based upon a simplified and more elegant version of this model, in which a BROWSER acts as the client requesting information from any one of millions of web servers.

.COM

Dot com, as it is spoken, is one of seven generic high-level DOMAIN names used originally to sort American addresses into broad categories. A .com address generally denotes a commercial organisation (contrasting with a .org address, for example, which theoretically indicates a non-profit organisation). Such addresses are considered to have a kudos greater than country-specific domains such as .co.uk. As a result, many individuals and small businesses have registered .com addresses; there were about 8m in mid-2000.

> *The open society, the unrestricted access to knowledge, the unplanned and uninhibited association of men for its furtherance – these are what may make a vast, complex, ever growing, ever changing, ever more specialised and expert technological world, nevertheless a world of human community.*
> J. Robert Oppenheimer

COMMUNITY

A collection of individuals or users of a website, MAILING LIST or NEWSGROUP, generally united through a common interest. Community-building is one of the biggest challenges faced by website owners, for whom unclicked BANNERS, empty CHAT rooms and discussion groups, or unclaimed web space presage doom. The rules for encouraging the development and retention of such communities are not clearly defined, and many theories circulate about how best to attempt this. Howard Rheingold's book *Virtual Communities,* available ONLINE, provides one of the best such discussions.

Broadly speaking, there are two types of online communities. Websites such as GEOCITIES and Tripod have built billion-dollar businesses by renting web space to anyone who wants it, organising people or businesses into neighbourhoods and creating a sense of place in an otherwise flat and sterile environment. More specifically, standalone commercial or special-interest sites use chat technology, moderated e-mail discussions, user forums and relationships with other sites to build audiences and encourage participation. Newsgroups, too, constitute communities in their own right, albeit ones whose discussions are unmoderated and whose members are less predictable in their movements and habits. Many of the principles behind successful community-building have their roots in organisations such as the WELL, one of the first online communities.

COMPRESSION

A technique for reducing the size of files, commonly used to speed transmission and DOWNLOAD times. Most compression algorithms work by removing or replacing redundant information from text or binary files, such as blank space or often-repeated characters. Picture files are especially suitable for compression, as they often contain large blocks of colour that can be represented in much simpler ways. Many picture formats, such as GIF and JPEG, are compressed. Popular compression formats for other forms of BINARY FILE include ZIP (the commonest form on PCs), ARC and TAR. Some compressed files are self-extracting; that is, they are combined with a program which automatically decompresses the contents of the files back into their original form.

COMPUSERVE

A pioneering ONLINE SERVICE. Compuserve has a special place in the hearts of Internet old-timers – for many it was their first experience of E-MAIL and CHAT. Originally conceived as a computer time-sharing service in 1969, the service expanded rapidly into a forum-based information resource of immense proportions. Widely used by computing professionals, Compuserve was the undisputed leader in online services for many years, despite its reliance on old proprietary technology, an arcane command-line interface and a clumsy subscriber ID system. The arrival of a WINDOWS-based interface made navigating the system somewhat easier, but despite a belated transition to ISP status it never achieved the mass appeal it hoped for. One possible reason for this is that H & R Block, Compuserve's owner for many years, was a firm of accountants. The company was sold to AOL in the early 1990s.

CONTENT

The constituent information of a website or other source. Content can take many forms, including text, sound, video, animation and numerical information. As many organisations have found, the process of accumulating content is expensive and time-consuming, irrespective of its subject. Few web users will pay for any of it as there is a vast amount of information available free on the web, and businesses that depend on the sale of content have been proved unrealistic time and time again. Even the biggest organisations have had their fingers burnt by the content issue. MICROSOFT, for example, was unable to persuade subscribers to its MSN service to pay for the content it offered separately.

People will pay for some kinds of specific content, such as archived magazine articles, detailed research from trusted sources and even some magazines. Generally, however, content is seen as way of attracting people to a website rather than a significant source of revenue in its own right.

The future will become vivid
Spreadsheets will crumble before creativity
Information will marry entertainment
They will have many children
Sony advertisement, *Wired* magazine

CONVERGENCE

The coming together of disparate technologies, such as Internet services, television and other forms of entertainment. Nearly everyone knows how to work a television set, but PCS are much harder for them to master. It makes sense, then, for the television to act as a central source of digital information, whether it be E-MAIL, the web, satellite and cable television, video-on-demand or video games.

There are, however, cultural problems associated with merging these technologies. For one thing, television-watching is a largely passive activity, whereas sending e-mail and playing games demand high degrees of interaction. Such issues have an impact on the design of devices handling these very different forms of information. There is a technical barrier, too, in that few homes have access to the high-speed cable, satellite or other digital networks necessary to make such integration feasible. Nevertheless, technology and media companies are investing heavily in bandwidth providers and set-top box manufacturers, in the hope of owning part or all of the consumer's connection.

COOKIE

A text file left by a website on a hard disk. Cookies record information about site visitors, especially information that can be used to make life easier for users on subsequent visits. When a visitor returns, the site retrieves the cookie and reads it for PASSWORD or LOGIN information, user-configured preferences such as page layout, or credit card numbers, for example. Advertisers and WEBMASTERS make extensive use of cookies to track the behaviour of site visitors, noting the sections and pages that they visit, keeping track of dead-ends that force users to go back on themselves and watching their response to BANNER advertising.

Sites that use cookies generally claim that their use is beneficial to users. But the mechanism by which cookies work is subject to criticism because of its invisibility. Unless told to do otherwise, BROWSERS accept cookies and share information without the user's awareness, raising concerns about security and privacy. Many people argue that the storing and transmission of browsing information is unethical, and fear that it may be sold to marketing organisations or retailers. Of particular concern is the use of cookies by SEARCH ENGINES to observe and analyse specific areas of interest. Some cookie critics have raised the possibility of cookies being used by law enforcement agencies to look into suspects' spheres of interest as evidence of illegal activities. These concerns are partly addressed by the OPEN PROFILING STANDARD, designed specifically to give users more control over the information they impart to websites.

C

COPYLEFT

A software licensing scheme in which programs can be modified, redistributed or even sold, with the proviso that anyone who does so also passes on the freedom to make further changes. The copyleft idea came from Richard Stallman, founder of the Free Software Foundation (FSF), in the collaborative spirit that created UNIX. It applies particularly to the FSF's GNU software. Unlike COPYRIGHT, copyleft favours the rights of users above those of commercial software makers, and ensures that anyone who wants to make improvements to the code for their own use or that of others can do so freely.

> *Copying all or parts of a program is as natural to a programmer as breathing, and as productive. It ought to be as free.*
> Richard M. Stallman

COPYRIGHT

The issue of who owns what on the Internet is, unsurprisingly, a complex one. Like obscenity laws, copyright laws differ from country to country, making regulation on the Internet difficult. The Internet has also thrown up some new and effectively ungovernable ways of distributing copyrighted material. A good example is the MP3 music format, which allows owners of CDs to copy and distribute CD-quality audio files by E-MAIL or on websites with little chance of being tracked down and prosecuted.

Organisations such as the World Intellectual Property Organisation (WIPO), one of the UN's specialised agencies and a forum for discussion and arbitration of copyright issues, have tried to garner support for new global copyright schemes, in particular protecting the content of DATABASES and the copies of material made during transmission over the Internet. Such proposals are not popular with academics and broadcasters dependent on research sources, or developing countries reliant on the continued influx of information from the developed world. Other initiatives, such as the Strategic Digital Music Initiative (SDMI), established by the music industry to prevent piracy of its works, have underestimated the resourcefulness of the net COMMUNITY and its intolerance of attempts to control its behaviour.

Discussions on these and other issues will continue for many years, and their resolution may take decades in an environment strange and unfamiliar to most copyright lawyers. It is clear that electronic media and the Internet in particular have raised previously unthought of issues concerning copyright, but legislation is getting tougher and copyright holders are becoming more aggressive in protecting their intellectual property. In the United States, the 1998 Digital Millennium Copyright Act, originally designed to protect digital works such as DVDs, has been used to force alleged music pirates to withdraw material from the NAPSTER music community. More significantly, MICROSOFT has invoked the act's powers to try to prevent criticism of one of its technical specifications, prompting many free-speech proponents and lawyers to declare the legislation seriously flawed. The fact remains that finding and prosecuting every copyright infringement on the net is a hugely daunting task for even the most tenacious officials, and that WIPO and other agencies have their work cut out for years ahead.

The question of intellectual property promises to be the Vietnam of the Internet.
Mitchell Kapor

CRACKER
Someone who breaks into someone else's computer system, usually on a NETWORK. Crackers may operate for profit, malice, ideology, braggadocio or plain old altruism; many have cracked systems simply to demonstrate security holes. Not to be confused with HACKER. (See also WAREZ.)

CRAWLER

A program that visits web pages and reads their contents, usually on behalf of a SEARCH ENGINE responding to a request from a website owner. Once read, the information is returned to the search engine, indexed and made generally available to the outside world. Most crawlers, also known as spiders or bots (short for robots, specialised kinds of AGENT), are well-behaved creatures that obey the Standard for Robot Exclusion, a set of guidelines governing the behaviour of such agents. Typically, a crawler will refer to a robots.txt file on each SERVER to identify no-go areas before doing its work. Some wait for gaps in server activity before accessing data, thus minimising their impact on server performance. A crawler cannot penetrate a FIREWALL, which limits its effectiveness.

CYBER-

A rather hackneyed prefix denoting a person, object or idea related to technology, especially that of the Internet and its culture. The term was introduced in 1948 by a scientist at the Massachusetts Institute of Technology (MIT), Norbert Weiner, who derived the word cybernetics from a Greek word meaning helmsman or governor to denote the new science of control systems. Its reappearance in popular culture can be traced to Doctor Who's cybermen, although it was most famously used in the term cyberspace, coined by William Gibson to describe the geography of the ONLINE world in his novel *Neuromancer*. It is now appropriated for use in many contemporary terms, including cybercafe, cybernaut, cyberpunk, cyberrights, cyberstalker and CYBERVENTING.

CYBERSQUATTING

The practice of acquiring a DOMAIN name with the intention of selling it on to a company or individual who wants to use it for their own purposes, especially those who feel their claim is more legitimate. The first-come, first-served nature of the domain name registration process and the lack of authentication by registrars mean that many companies have found the domains they wanted for their web presences have been bought by quick-thinking entrepreneurs. Some companies have had success in reclaiming domains they see as their rightful property, notably MTV and McDonalds, but many others have found it cheaper and easier simply to pay up and move on.

Despite the efforts of organisations such as the International Trademark Association, which has campaigned for new international legislation on cybersquatting, the issues surrounding it are unlikely to be resolved soon. Part of the problem is that unlike the real world, where companies with the same name have generally coexisted happily for decades, the web demands unique identifiers for addresses. No process exists for settling disputes over this kind of intellectual property, although REALNAMES makes an attempt to determine who has the right to use particular names on its alternative web navigation system. Leoblair.com was registered very soon after baby Leo's birth.

CYBERVENTING
Letting off steam about your employer, boss or colleagues in public, usually on a website designed for the purpose. Many such sites now exist, from the well-balanced www.workingwounded.com to the rather more vituperative www.mybosssucks.com, and some companies such as Walmart have sites devoted entirely to their perceived inadequacies as employers or businesses. Although many employees feel better after a good cybervent, some have been tracked down and even fired by their bosses, especially after revealing confidential information.

CYBRARIAN
A librarian or researcher specialising in the Internet, rather than books, as a source of information.

CYPHERPUNK
Someone dedicated to the use of cryptography to build anonymous, private communications

systems. Members of the cypherpunk movement were responsible for cracking the first RSA-encrypted message in 1994, revealing weaknesses in the system and helping to raise awareness of the issues surrounding the ENCRYPTION debate. Cryptographic systems created by cypherpunks are freely available for others to modify and use.

D

DATABASE

A computerised filing system forming the core of most corporate computer systems. Databases are, on the face of it, simple tools used to store and retrieve information. In reality, they are big and complex programs that are subjected to extreme pressure as the demand for sophisticated analysis of corporate data grows. Until fairly recently databases handled only numbers and text, but the acceptance of MULTIMEDIA technologies has added a requirement for storage of more complex forms of data such as video and graphics.

Databases are commonly used as the engines driving websites. Retail sites, for example, use databases to store the details of their customers (a non-trivial task in the case of companies like AMAZON, which have tens of millions of them) and the items they have for sale, and many sites now use database technology to manage the display of editorial CONTENT. The most common form in current use is the relational database, which stores and indexes information in multiple tables, although some small businesses use much simpler flat-file databases to store their key data. The importance of database technology to the Internet world is reflected in the massive growth of companies like Oracle.

Database technology is well understood, and the real challenge for database owners in the digital age is to maintain control and ownership of the facts their databases contain. Most European countries give database-builders some ownership rights. In the United States, however, the courts have ruled that facts are not subject to COPYRIGHT laws as there is no authorship involved in their collection or creation; they are, simply, facts. This means that a START-UP supplier of telephone directories can legally copy entries from a competitor's directories, for example. This makes database builders understandably nervous in an age when digital information can be copied swiftly and invisibly. An American attempt to extend the scope of European laws to the United States at the 1996 WIPO meeting in Geneva met with failure,

D

after intensive lobbying from scientists, broadcasters, researchers and Internet companies worried about their sources drying up.

DATA MINING

A set of techniques for sifting through huge amounts of information held in DATABASES, with the aim of discerning useful trends, facts or associations. Data mining is used by retailers, especially supermarkets, to discover previously unsuspected buying patterns of particular customers or demographic groups; people who always buy fish on Fridays, for example, or the probably apocryphal nappies-and-beer phenomenon said to be demonstrated by reluctant shopping fathers. They can then use the information so gleaned to target these people for special offers or specific products.

The fiercest critics of data mining are privacy campaigners, who say that it subjects people to involuntary examination of their lives and represents a serious threat to freedom. In the United States, data mining techniques were famously used to identify the alcohol-buying patterns of a man who made an injury claim against a supermarket after slipping on its floors; the implication being that he was probably drunk at the time of the accident. (The supermarket's evidence was thrown out.)

DATA WAREHOUSE

A collection of DATABASES combining information from different parts of an organisation, generally used in conjunction with DATA MINING techniques. A large retailer's data warehouse, for example, may contain information about customer purchases, supplier deliveries, transport vehicle schedules and new products. Such information is used to improve supply chain management, target customers more effectively and plan the introduction of new ranges of goods. Theoretically, such warehouses improve a company's internal and external communications, allowing staff to share information more efficiently and outside partners to become more tightly integrated with the business.

DAY TRADER

A usually fanatical amateur stockmarket enthusiast who trades from a PC, perhaps as many as 50 times a day. Day traders are viewed with animosity by some investment professionals, who have accused them of distorting the stockmarket and causing volatility in share prices. Their very existence is a tribute to the democratising power of the Internet, comes the reply. On the net anyone can be a trader, not just the elite. Many of them, however, must now be wishing they had stuck to more traditional investments. A study by American securities regulators in the state of Washington found that 77% of day traders lose money.

DEMON INTERNET

The first ISP in the UK to offer full dial-up Internet access to consumers. Demon Internet's "tenner-a-month" pricing policy and its full range of Internet services established the model for British ISPs, which was only recently superseded by free-access providers such as FREESERVE. Founded in 1992, Demon started with modest ambitions, aiming for 200 members in its first year and 4,500 by the end of 1995, a figure it exceeded by a factor of 10. By May 1998 the total number of subscribers exceeded 180,000. The company was sold to Scottish Power for £66m later that year. In April 2000 Demon agreed to pay damages to Laurence Godfrey, who took action against the company for refusing to remove allegedly libellous comments about him from NEWSGROUP postings. The case caused some panic in the British ISP community, for whom the prospect of being held responsible for the content of over 1m newsgroup messages a day is not a welcome one.

DENIAL OF SERVICE ATTACK

Describes a particular form of electronic attack against a website or other digital service, which results in the temporary loss of service and access to resources. Such attacks rarely damage data or equipment, but they can be expensive for their targets, especially if the attack is prolonged. In February 2000, some of the world's largest websites, including YAHOO, AMAZON and EBAY, were forced offline for several hours by such attacks.

Denial of service (DOS) attacks are almost always made by malicious CRACKERS. They usually involve the sending of vast amounts of data across the Internet to a SERVER that is not equipped to deal with it, either from a single computer or, more commonly, a widely distributed group of computers that have been programmed to attack a particular site at the same time. Some targets have reported that servers were being flooded with as much as 1 gigabyte of data per second, which clearly points to a determined effort by a third party to cause a disruption. Other companies have been accused of crying DOS attack to mask server crashes and other self-generated errors, in the hope of diverting attention away from serious internal problems. Many kinds of DOS attack are known, including the SYN, Teardrop and Smurf varieties.

DES
Data Encryption Standard, a widely used method of data ENCRYPTION judged so difficult to break by the US government that its export to other countries was prohibited. Based on a 1970s IBM algorithm called Lucifer, DES was adopted as an official standard by the US government in 1977. It uses a PRIVATE KEY method, in which one of 72 quadrillion keys is used to encode and decode a message. A sample DES message was cracked in June 1997 by DESCHALL, a project involving thousands of people and computers linked by the Internet using a brute force attack to test all the possible keys. (See DISTRIBUTED COMPUTING.)

DHTML
Dynamic Hypertext Mark-up Language, a collective term for the combination of advanced HTML features, style sheets and scripting. Used together,

these elements allow the contents of a web page to change after the page has loaded, without the need for complex programming or reference back to the web SERVER. Often-seen examples include text paragraphs or images changing colour and shape when the mouse is moved over them, although it can be used for more sophisticated animation or drag-and-drop effects. DHTML is built around the W3C's Document Object Model (DOM), in which each element of a web page, such as a heading, paragraph or IMAGE, is viewed as an object that can be controlled using JAVASCRIPT or VBSCRIPT.

DIGERATI
Movers and shakers in the digital world, especially those celebrated in John Brockman's book of the same name.

DIGITAL DIVIDE
A term used to describe the imbalance in access to information technology among diverse social groups. Although this divide is most apparent in developing countries, where only the rich and well-connected have access to even the simplest types of communication such as telephones and fax machines, a 1999 American government study entitled "*Falling Through the Net: Defining the Digital Divide*" found that it is still apparent even in more affluent societies. American households with incomes of over $75,000 were over 20 times more likely to have access to the Internet than those at the lowest income levels and nine times more likely to have a computer at home. The divide appears to be growing rather than shrinking across income and ethnic groups.

DIGITAL REVOLUTION
An expression coined by *Wired* magazine to describe the transformation being wrought by technology in all aspects of our lives.

DIGITAL SIGNATURE
A device that uniquely identifies the sender of an

electronic message or document, based on PUBLIC KEY CRYPTOGRAPHY. The purpose of a digital signature is to guarantee that senders of such messages really are who they claim to be, an increasingly important concern for businesses considering E-COMMERCE strategies. Without such signatures it is hard to be sure that an E-MAIL is not forged or that a web-based vendor of goods and services is trustworthy.

Digital signatures are issued by certificate authorities such as Verisign, an American company specialising in authenticating the digital identity of people and organisations. Typically, a signature will contain the user's name, a serial number, expiry dates and a copy of the certificate holder's public key. It also contains the signature of the issuing authority to verify that the certificate itself is real.

DISINTERMEDIATION
The process by which producers and consumers are brought closer together, making middlemen redundant. This ugly word, borrowed from the banking world, is especially relevant to Internet technologies which allow their users direct access to information that might otherwise require a mediator. Examples include medical and legal websites, which may bypass the need for real doctors and lawyers or at least change the relationship with them.

Any business model that relies upon disintermediation ignores the fact that most of the successful Internet companies work in precisely the opposite way, acting as INFOMEDIARIES rather than disintermediators. AMAZON and EBAY, for example, both bring buyers and sellers together; they are middlemen, albeit of a sophisticated kind.

DISTRIBUTED COMPUTING
Describes a way of using networked computers to work together collaboratively, using the combined power of their processors to perform large or difficult tasks. Computers attached to the Internet have been used for distributed computing projects,

perhaps most notably in the cracking of ENCRYPTION algorithms such as DES and RSA – tasks which might take thousands or even millions of years on a single computer. Other applications include the use of networked machines to generate and render complex graphics, such as those used in modern films, or to search for signals from alien civilisations in radio-astronomy data.

DNS

See DOMAIN NAME SYSTEM

DOCUVERSE

A description of the HYPERTEXT world envisaged by Ted Nelson (see XANADU).

DOMAIN

One or more computers on the Internet that are described by a particular name and IP address. For example, computers that are attached to the network at *The Economist* are within the domain economist.com. Domains and their names are organised hierarchically by the domain name system (DNS). At the top of this hierarchy are the top-level domains (TLDs) seen at the end of an Internet address, such as .COM, .uk or .net. Below these are the names of specific institutions or parts thereof within that group, such as "economist", and lastly a name referring to a specific machine, such as "www". The whole constitutes an Internet address that uses easily memorable, recognisable letters and words instead of numbers; www.economist.com is a good example.

The administration of the domain system is a complex business involving a mix of quasi-public organisations, registries for individual TLDs and private companies acting as registrars. Exactly who has the right to assign and manage domain names, and who should profit from that arrangement, is still under discussion. Another well-publicised problem is that of cybersquatting – the appropriation of a domain name resembling another company's trademark, usually in the hope of selling it at a profit.

DOMAIN NAME SYSTEM

The means by which domains are organised on the Internet. DNS is also the means by which a DOMAIN name (such as www.economist.com) is translated into the IP ADDRESS (such as 165.117.52.149) used to find and identify an Internet location. Lists of domain names and their corresponding addresses are distributed throughout the Internet on DNS SERVERS.

In May 2000, there were nearly 16m unique domain names registered worldwide. At the beginning of the year over 400,000 new registrations were being added each week.

DOOM

A violent computer game created by id Software. Doom was the first game to exploit the try-before-you-buy software distribution model now accepted as standard practice by thousands of software companies. Instead of buying the whole game unseen, players could download the first third of the game free of charge from websites and BULLETIN BOARDS, providing a teaser which proved irresistible to millions of gamers around the world.

id's creation was largely responsible for the popularity of ONLINE GAMING. Designed originally for solo play, it also included multiplayer facilities for LOCAL AREA NETWORKS. Its successor, Quake, added Internet-based play, allowing anyone with a net connection to join games on one of hundreds of Quake servers worldwide. Nearly all contemporary games now offer similar facilities.

DOT COM

The spoken version of .COM.

DOT-COMMERY

The engagement in new kinds of Internet-based commercial activity, usually by people leaving jobs in traditional businesses to form their own START-UPS.

DOWNLOAD

To transfer information from a remote computer, such as a website or mail SERVER, to a local computer's hard disk across a NETWORK or MODEM connection. (See also UPLOAD.)

DSL

Digital Subscriber Line (or, sometimes, Loop). DSL services are designed to improve BANDWIDTH connections over ordinary copper phone lines. A number of variants exist, each with a different initial, so it is sometimes known generically as XDSL. The best known, and the one closest to becoming widely available in Europe and the United States, is ADSL; others include CDSL, SDSL, RADSL, HDSL, VDSL.

DUNGEON

See MUD.

DWELLTIME

The time a website visitor can be persuaded to spend hanging around looking at advertisements, a quantity closely related to the site's STICKINESS. Although many studies have been made of the average visitor's dwelltime, few have managed to suggest practical ways of increasing it. The problem has got worse as the amount of free information on the web has grown; the less useful or relevant that information is, the faster dwelltime moves towards zero. The problem is especially severe for PORTAL sites, which have a conflict between keeping people on the site long enough to see the ADVERTISING and being useful enough to serve as a jumping-off point for exploring the rest of the web.

E-

Short for electronic. Almost as tired as CYBER-, the e- prefix is now used extensively to describe new, digital forms of old practices: E-MAIL, E-COMMERCE, e-tailing, e-zine.

EBAY

See ONLINE AUCTION.

E-BOOK

A generic term for electronic books, in essence devices designed to replace printed pages with electronic equivalents. Several such products are now available, all of them tablet computers with flat-screen LCD displays to which the text of books, magazines or other documents can be downloaded from Internet sites as and when they are required. E-books' proponents argue that this ability to reuse them again and again will in time spell the end of the paper-based book as we know it. Critics cite the poor readability of the screen, the weight of the devices, their limited battery life and their incompatibility with bathtubs as reasons to avoid them.

Some of these technical issues will inevitably be solved over time. MICROSOFT, for example, has developed new screen font technology called ClearType to help make screens more readable; and Joseph Jacobson, an assistant professor at Massachusetts Institute of Technology (MIT), is working on a project that uses "digital ink" to display text and pictures on turnable pages. More important than any of this is the question of whether the deeply entrenched symbolic power of books in our culture can be replicated by a few ounces of silicon and plastic. Most observers agree that the bookless library is about as likely to happen as the paperless office: that is to say, not at all.

E-BUSINESS

Another term for E-COMMERCE.

E-CASH

Electronic money. E-cash can be stored and spent in a number of ways, which generally involve storing digital tokens representing dollars, pounds or any other currency in some sort of electronic medium, such as a smart card or an electronic wallet on a computer's hard disk. Anyone wanting to spend money transfers these tokens to the recipient's electronic piggy bank, either by transmitting them across an Internet connection or by handing over the smart card.

E-cash's principal advantages are the speed and security of the transactions it allows. There are hundreds of e-cash systems in commercial development, and companies such as Mondex have conducted consumer trials in the UK, the United States and Europe. Each uses its own complex blend of ENCRYPTION technologies, including DIGITAL SIGNATURES and systems such as SSL and SET, which make it hard for unauthorised people to intercept payments or break into electronic storage mechanisms.

E-COMMERCE

Broadly, the buying and selling of goods and services on the Internet. With the possible exception of PORNOGRAPHY, no other area of the Internet has attracted more attention than retail e-commerce. The rise of companies like AMAZON and EBAY has alerted the public to the possibilities of electronic shopping. The real money, though, is likely to be made in the business sector, where new entities such as the INFOMEDIARY are likely to stimulate new kinds of business by bringing together buyers and sellers in previously impossible ways.

EDI

Electronic Data Interchange, a standard way of exchanging data between companies that predates the Internet. It is especially suitable for sharing information such as prices or parts numbers. EDI has been used widely in the corporate world for nearly a decade, and now is being integrated into some Internet technologies (see EXTRANET).

EFF

Electronic Frontier Foundation, a non-profit organisation that campaigns for ONLINE civil liberties. Founded in 1990 by John Perry Barlow and Mitch Kapor, the EFF is a loud voice against CENSORSHIP and an influential supporter of free speech and privacy.

E-MAIL

Short for electronic mail, an electronic message sent from one computer to another.

EMOTICON

A short string of ASCII characters used to add an expression of emotion to an E-MAIL or other ONLINE message. Most emoticons are designed to represent a simplified facial expression such as a smile (hence the alternative name "smiley") or a frown. So :-) is used to signify amusement either at someone else's wit or, at least as often, the author's own. Emoticons are regarded somewhat snootily by the net's self-appointed intelligentsia, for whom they symbolise the death of irony and clarity of expression. :-(

ENCODER

A program that converts data from one form to another, often with the aim of reducing its size. In digital audio technology the best-known example is an MP3 encoder, which converts a sound recording (usually in the WINDOWS WAV format) into a much smaller, but still near-CD quality, MP3 file. Other COMPRESSION techniques use similar encoders. An important exception to the size-shrinking rule is the UUENCODE algorithm used by E-MAIL programs to convert an ATTACHMENT into a format that can be understood (via a decoding process) by any recipient of the message. Uuencoded messages are usually bigger than the originals.

ENCRYPTION

The conversion of a message or data file into a form that cannot be understood by unauthorised readers. Encryption is the technology that makes E-COMMERCE possible because it underlies the security systems used to protect electronic financial transactions. Many forms of encryption exist, ranging from simple ciphers such as ROT13 to intricate mathematical algorithms.

Whatever their level of complexity, all encryption techniques require at least one KEY, which describes how a message is encoded and how it can be decoded. Single-key systems, usually called secret key or PRIVATE KEY encryption, are used by algorithms such as DES. The problem with single-key systems is that if the private key held by the sender and recipient of a message falls into the wrong hands, it can quickly be used to decipher any message. It also requires a separate key for every transaction or business partner, so anyone trying to build an e-commerce-based business must generate millions of different private keys and then find ways of sending them securely over the Internet – an impractical task.

So far, the best solution to this problem is PUBLIC KEY ENCRYPTION, which relies on a two-key system. To send a private message, the recipient's public key, which can be listed in the equivalent of a phone directory or on a website, is used to encrypt it. Once so encrypted, only the private key held by the recipient will reveal the contents of the message. A DIGITAL SIGNATURE works the other way round, being encrypted with the sender's private key and decrypted with their public key.

Keys are complex entities, and their usefulness is directly proportional to their size. The bigger the key, the more secure – "stronger" – is the encryption. Key size is measured in BITS, and those measured in tens of bits are regarded as easily crackable with today's powerful computers; those over 1,000 bits long are effectively unbreakable. The problem facing many would-be users of such strong encryption software is that governments are doing their best to restrict its use, claiming that it will place terrorists, drug smugglers and paedophiles beyond the reach of the law. So keen are they to be able to continue their eavesdropping activities that some have legislated against the use of strong encryption. Governments generally favour KEY ESCROW schemes, which require users of encryption to hand over copies of their private keys to a TRUSTED THIRD PARTY.

Such measures are probably doomed to failure because they ignore the fact that strong encryption technologies – the PGP program is a good example – are already widely available on the Internet, often at little or no cost. The UK government has been rethinking its initial enthusiasm for key escrow schemes following widespread concern that such schemes would severely undermine confidence in e-commerce. Meanwhile, the US government announced plans to relax export restrictions on encryption software in late 1999.

EUDORA

A long-established E-MAIL program, especially popular among Apple Macintosh users.

EXTRAMERCIAL

A type of advertisement seen on web pages, which scrolls down the right-hand side of a page in response to a click on a button. Extramercials are seen as an improvement on standard BANNER advertisements, because they provide more space in which advertisers can describe and illustrate their wares. Some sites have reported three times as many CLICKTHROUGHS on extramercials as conventional banners and have thus been able to raise their prices, with a corresponding much-needed increase in revenue.

EXTRANET

A NETWORK built on standard Internet technology, typically used by an organisation to share information with customers, suppliers and other business partners. An extranet is generally an extension of a company's INTRANET, modified to allow access by specified external users.

Although they are based on standard Internet technology, extranets are much harder to build than this simple description suggests. One problem is security, an important issue when considering what sort of data to make available, so FIREWALLS, DIGITAL SIGNATURES and message-level ENCRYPTION are commonly used. A potentially bigger problem is that of standardising data formats and business processes across organisations. Industry standards such as EDI and, increasingly, XML are important parts of the solution to this problem.

FAQ

Frequently Asked Questions. Most NEWSGROUPS contain a self-explanatory list of questions and answers designed to guide newcomers, which will also explain the purpose of the group and give guidelines for posting messages. For reasons of NETIQUETTE (and self-preservation), it is a good idea to read the FAQ before posting questions such as: "What's this newsgroup all about then?" Repeating an oft-asked question without consulting the FAQ is likely to attract at least one FLAME.

FIBRE OPTIC

A fine glass fibre that transmits light, sometimes known as optical fibre or just fibre. Fibre optic cables transmit data much faster than copper wires and are much less susceptible to electromagnetic interference. Most long-distance telephone and Internet traffic travels across fibre, which now connects nearly all telephone exchanges and forms most Internet BACKBONES. The first transatlantic fibre optic cable, laid in 1988, can carry nearly 38,000 simultaneous telephone conversations.

Much has been made of the potential benefits of "bringing fibre to the kerb" by replacing the existing copper wires on which telephone systems are currently based and linking the fast fibre connection to the home using standard coaxial cable. However, fibre optic technology is costly to install, and the widespread availability of local fibre is still a long way off. It needs considerably more physical protection than existing wires. Meanwhile, technologies such as ADSL are demonstrating that copper still has plenty of life left in it.

FILE SERVER

A computer responsible for the central storage and management of data files that can be accessed by other computers on the same NETWORK. File servers are typically equipped with large, fast hard disks for rapid transfer of information, as well as lots of memory and often more than one processor. (See SERVER.)

FILTER

A program (or part of a program) that examines a message for specified criteria and then processes it accordingly. A good example is represented by the rules in many E-MAIL packages that allow a user to determine what happens to each incoming mail message. For example, e-mail from anybody at economist.com can be automatically placed in a folder called "Economist", or all messages without subjects can be deleted without being read. Filtering is also used extensively by BLOCKING SOFTWARE programs.

FINGER

A program for determining the name associated with an E-MAIL address, originally developed as part of BSD (Berkeley System Distribution) variant of UNIX. Finger programs can either be run on a local computer or be accessed via one of many finger GATEWAYS on the Internet. These programs locate a finger SERVER associated with the DOMAIN at which the e-mail address is located. This server holds name information and, optionally, other personalised information about the user of that address. Many universities and large organisations maintain finger servers, as do some ISPS.

FIREWALL

A system composed of both hardware and software that enforces access control between two networks, usually between a private LOCAL AREA NETWORK and the public Internet. Most firewalls are installed to prevent unauthorised access to networks by potentially malicious outsiders, although they are often used in corporate environments to control the use of Internet resources by employees. A new breed of firewall has emerged that protects individual Internet users from CRACKERS armed with PORT SCANNERS.

Firewalls are flexible tools that can be configured to provide security at many levels. Some allow only E-MAIL traffic, for example, and others block only incoming traffic from specific sites or services. They also provide important logging and auditing functions, allowing administrators to see how much and what sort of traffic passed across the NETWORK, how many illegal access attempts were made and even where those attempts came from – a potentially useful way of tracking down intruders.

Because of their general usefulness firewalls are often seen as the last word in network security, and they are thus regularly installed as a sort of corporate security blanket for concerned management. They are only as good as an overall security policy, however, a fact that many companies have ignored to their cost. No firewall can prevent an employee walking out of the building with a bag full of corporate data stored on disk or tape; equally, it may not be able to protect a network that allows dial-up access to a MODEM pool. Firewalls also provide poor protection against VIRUSES, which are often concealed in compressed or encrypted files.

FLAME

An abusive communication from a fellow Internet user, usually in a NEWSGROUP but sometimes by E-MAIL or in a CHAT forum. Many things can trigger a flame. Common causes are failure to observe NETIQUETTE, ignorance of a FAQ and simple stupidity, or intemperance on either side. Flames often induce considerable shock in first-time recipients, who may be surprised by the vehemence and forthrightness of the attack. Braver individuals may respond in kind, which may ultimately result in escalation to a full-scale flame war. Such frank exchanges of views are generally discouraged by the local COMMUNITY, but they can be tremendous fun for a LURKER.

FLASH

A popular software package used by web developers to create glitzy effects and animations on web pages. Many people use Flash technology to create slick, animated interfaces for their sites, largely because of the speed at which its graphical effects download even across comparatively slow connections. Flash-enabled sites often include high-quality music and interactive features as well as just pretty graphics.

404 NOT FOUND

An error message generated by a website. 404 errors occur when a URL or a LINK from another web page is either wrong or has changed for some reason, and the page cannot then be found. The number itself is an HTTP status code, established by Tim Berners-Lee as part of the original HTTP specification. The 404 Not Found message has a special place in the hearts of web users because of its ubiquitous and often unforgiving nature. At its most prosaic, the message simply appears in text form. More imaginative site owners have embellished it to include an animation, a haiku or a philosophical treatise on the meaning of 404 – not necessarily what you were looking for, but sometimes amusing nonetheless. Much to the consternation of web GEEKS everywhere, the future of 404 messages is threatened by version 5 of MICROSOFT'S INTERNET EXPLORER BROWSER, which hijacks 404 pages and replaces them with its own useful but rather soulless advice.

FRAME RELAY

A high-speed PACKET-SWITCHED network PROTOCOL, often used in local and wide area networks. Unlike other packet-switched connections, which use data segments of fixed size, frame relay connections put data into variable-sized units (called frames) before transmission. Delivery of these frames can be prioritised, so that companies can choose levels of service quality in which some frames are deemed more important than others. Frame relay connections take advantage of unused BANDWIDTH to optimise data transmission, via a special circuit called a permanent virtual circuit (PVC). PVCs provide many of the benefits of an always-on LEASED LINE without the associated high cost, but they are not ideally suited to voice and video transmission.

FREE SOFTWARE FOUNDATION

An organisation dedicated to eliminating restrictions on copying, redistribution and modification of computer software. Founded by Richard Stallman in 1983, the Free Software Foundation (FSF) develops and distributes GNU, a UNIX-like OPERATING SYSTEM that can be freely modified by users within the provisions of the COPYLEFT system. (See also LINUX.)

FREEMAIL

Any form of free E-MAIL service, especially one that is web-based. Freemail services such as Hotmail and Rocketmail have been extremely successful as they enable anyone with access to a BROWSER to have their own e-mail account. Often used by students and travellers, freemail is also popular with people who need to keep business and personal e-mail accounts separate.

Despite their low-rent image, freemail accounts are broadly equal in capability to traditional POP-based accounts, with the added advantage that they make it possible to pick up e-mail from almost any machine in the world with an Internet connection. Most provide the ability to FILTER incoming mail, send and receive ATTACHMENTS, maintain an ONLINE address book, copy messages to multiple recipients and even retrieve mail from POP accounts.

There are, inevitably, some problems with freemail. Performance is generally much slower than POP, as SERVERS are often heavily loaded and it takes longer for messages to DOWNLOAD. More worrying for unwary users is security, especially on shared machines, as incoming mail is stored in the browser's CACHE and can often be accessed by anyone with a little browser knowledge. The issue that matters most, however, is that mail is free only as long as the provider is in service – not something easily guaranteed in the turbulent Internet marketplace.

FREESERVE

A UK-based ISP that provides free Internet access

to its subscribers. Freeserve was founded in late 1998 by Dixons, a high-street retailing group. Within six months of launch it was the biggest ISP in the UK, easily overtaking stalwarts of many years' standing such as DEMON and AOL. Unlike most ISPs, which charge a flat fee or an hourly rate for Internet access, Freeserve earns money from the telephone calls to the service itself and to its premium-rate technical support line. Freeserve's revenue is shared with Energis, the company's supplier of BANDWIDTH. Some additional income is generated by ADVERTISING on the service's PORTAL.

Freeserve's success triggered a revolution in the ISP business in the UK, with many existing companies abolishing their monthly fees and many others starting new free services. But one serious drawback to the free ISP model, the low barrier to exit, has contributed to concern in the investment community about its sustainability. Freeserve's initial public share offering, in July 1999, was massively oversubscribed. By late 1999 there were several hundred free ISPs in the UK, and the model was catching on fast in Europe and the United States. The long-term success of these ventures depends largely on their ability to attract new growth (and thus new advertising); a tricky proposition in a crowded market where it is easy to become a new player.

FTP

File Transfer Protocol, a standard way for computers on the Internet to exchange files. Like HTTP, FTP programs use the TCP/IP protocols on which the Internet is based to manage the transmission of BINARY FILES from one place to another. Many HTML authors use FTP to transfer web page files to their web SERVER, and it is commonly used to DOWNLOAD programs and other binary files from host computers on the Internet. Most browsers are capable of downloading files using FTP.

GATEWAY

A device connecting different networks, especially those using different standards or PROTOCOLS. Gateways are an essential part of the Internet, as they allow systems that know nothing about each to other exchange information. A good example is an E-MAIL gateway which connects two different proprietary e-mail systems, allowing the users of each to communicate as if they were on the same NETWORK. Gateways typically reside on a dedicated SERVER, which may also host a FIREWALL and PROXY SERVER.

GEEK

Traditionally, someone whose fascination for technology overwhelms all other pursuits, with all the negative stereotypes this implies; in short, a NERD. For most of the history of personal computers the term was derogatory, but geekdom, especially of the Internet variety, has now become stylish. Nearly all the people who have built high-profile Internet businesses are geeks of one kind or another – evidence, perhaps, that the geek shall indeed inherit the earth.

GEOCITIES

One of the best examples of COMMUNITY-building on a large scale on the Internet. Geocities is home to thousands of individual websites, organised by "neighbourhoods" with names such as Hollywood and SoHo. Members are referred to as homesteaders, and are accorded facilities luxurious even by Internet giveaway-culture standards: free web space, free E-MAIL addresses, free tools for building sites and an almost endless array of bells and whistles for personalising a HOME PAGE.

A price for this benevolence was set in 1999, when YAHOO bought Geocities for $5 billion. Members seeking to modify their sites after the takeover discovered that they had first to agree to a revised set of terms and conditions. This meant that Yahoo effectively owned the CONTENT of their sites and could do with it what it wished. This unpopular strategy resulted in a mass defection of members to a Boycott Yahoo site and a lot of bad publicity for Yahoo.

43% of Internet users are American. Only about half of 1% are Indian, despite outnumbering Americans by nearly four to one. By the year 2002, 490m people around the world will have Internet access.

GET BIG FAST

An E-COMMERCE mantra first attributed to Jeff Bezos, CEO of AMAZON.com, and the title of a book of the same name. Bezos is said to have distributed T-shirts with this slogan at the first company picnic in 1996, and his idea that the scale of his business would be a critical part of its success has been adopted by many other Internet START-UPS. Some have suggested that a version more appropriate in today's climate might be "Get Bought Fast".

GIF

Graphics Interchange Format. GIF files are INTER-LACED graphics files widely used on the web, especially for simple computer-generated pictures and animations but also for digital photographs. Most BANNERS are in GIF form. In 1994 COMPUSERVE, the owner of the GIF specification, decided to make software developers pay for the privilege of including GIF support in their programs, which dismayed many who had considered GIF a free and open standard. More recently Unisys, owner of the COMPRESSION patents on which GIF is based, has tried to extract payment from small software developers and anyone using "unauthorised" GIF files on their sites, an even less popular move that resulted in the Burn All GIFs campaign in 1999. Despite this, GIF is likely to remain an industry standard even in the face of the technical superiority of alternatives such as PNG and JPEG, because it is the only common graphics format that supports animation.

G

GOPHER

A PROTOCOL used to find information on the Internet. Search programs such as Veronica consult Gopher SERVERS containing hierarchically organised information stored in text files, which can be referenced by subject. Gopher is said to be named after the mascot of the University of Minnesota, where it was originally developed. For many years Gopher provided the easiest way to find information on the Internet, but its popularity has declined with the advent of web technology. Nonetheless, many of the original archives survive, especially in universities, and can be accessed with most web BROWSERS. Gopher is still used extensively by specialist researchers looking for information not accessible to the main SEARCH ENGINES.

GRAND CENTRAL STATION

AGENT software, developed by IBM, which continuously searches data sources for specified information that can be delivered to a PC or PDA. Written in JAVA, it works with web SERVERS, NEWSGROUPS, FTP sites, DATABASE systems and even corporate presentations and E-MAIL archives to find information as soon as it becomes available, rather than later.

GROUPWARE

Software that helps people work together more productively and share knowledge more efficiently. The groupware concept was popularised in the early 1990s by NOTES, a product developed by Lotus Development (creator of the famous 1-2-3 spreadsheet). It has since been embraced by nearly every vendor of software that allows more than one user, including NOVELL, MICROSOFT, NETSCAPE and a host of smaller companies.

Some groupware products have a broad generic scope that helps with simple office automation tasks and the sharing of resources. Others have much more specialised roles in markets such as computer-aided design (CAD), where it is important for people to be able to collaborate on drawings and diagrams. Even word processors and BROWSERS are now packed with groupware features; the former for aiding multiple contributions to documents, the latter for building sophisticated mailing lists and discussion groups. One of the most important applications is scheduling, an area where once-simple personal information management software has mutated into big, complex programs for planning meetings, building resources and managing multiple diaries.

Generally, these applications rely on expensive proprietary technology, and are thus threatened by the more open and flexible possibilities offered by Internet standards. INTRANETS, in particular, are much cheaper than large-scale Notes installations and generally more flexible. From there, it is a short step to an EXTRANET capable of embracing customers, suppliers and business partners. With this in mind, companies such as Lotus have been forced to lower their costs and add TCP/IP-based features to their existing products.

Groupware is viewed with some suspicion by companies committed to old-style hierarchical management teams. Like a NEWSGROUP, it often fosters an electronic soapbox mentality, encouraging employees to express views they might keep to themselves in more traditional face-to-face environments. Reaching any sort of consensus using groupware tools can be a challenge, and many systems are thus used primarily as decision-support tools for senior management rather than free-for-all company-wide discussion groups.

GSM

Global System for Mobile communications, a standard for digital mobile telephones widely used in Europe. GSM and its variants are rapidly being adopted elsewhere in the world, especially in Asia and Australasia. GSM allows phones to send and receive data at up to 9,600bps in conjunction with a personal computer or PDA. It is not generally suitable for surfing websites designed to be accessed by PCs, but it is adequate for E-MAIL and text-only websites that have been designed with low-BANDWIDTH connections in mind. The growth of tailored web applications using WML should improve the Internet capability of GSM devices. A third-generation version of GSM, due within two years, will massively increase the available bandwidth, making it suitable for much more data-intensive applications.

HACKER

Broadly, someone who enjoys exploring, using and extending technology, particularly but not exclusively computer technology. This is to simplify the issue, however, and debate persists over what a hacker is and who qualifies for membership of the essentially meritocratic hacker community. Some people consider that to be a true hacker a person must be an enthusiastic programmer, preferably for the UNIX OPERATING SYSTEM. Others maintain that an expert or enthusiast of any kind qualifies. Perhaps the most useful definition is simply someone who enjoys intellectual challenges and creative problem-solving, especially within the context of technology. One generally recognised truth is that people who call themselves hackers are probably not – the honour is conferred by their peers rather than by the individuals themselves.

The word is often used to describe someone who is actually a CRACKER, which enrages the hacker community. As Eric Raymond says in his enlightening essay "How To Become A Hacker", "hackers build things, crackers break them". And build things they do: UNIX, USENET, the WORLD WIDE WEB and the Internet itself are all the work of hackers.

> *I want to get to know the hacker community better. These people are America's future.*
> Jeffrey Hunker, US National Security Council

HDML

Handheld Devices Mark-up Language (see WML).

HELPER APPLICATION

A program used by a BROWSER to display or play particular files. In their original incarnations, browsers understood only HTML, GIF and JPEG files. So if a web page contained anything else, such as an audio file, a special program was needed to handle it. These programs were usually supplied by the user and ran separately from the browser.

In later browsers many helper functions are handled by the browser itself or by a PLUG-IN, but some file types, such as MP3, still need separate helpers.

HIT

A single request for a file as logged by a web SERVER. When a BROWSER requests an HTML page, the server must deliver not just the HTML code but any associated objects such as IMAGE files. Each one of these counts as a hit, so a single web page with nine images – common enough, given the number of graphical elements used for design and NAVIGATION purposes in a typical web page – will generate ten hits. Hits are therefore a good indicator of the amount of work a server is doing but an unreliable measure of how many pages are actually being viewed. In the early days of the web disingenuous marketers used hits as a measure of a site's popularity. People (especially advertisers) have seen through this ruse and IMPRESSIONS are now the measure of choice.

When I took office, only high energy physicists had ever heard of what is now called the World Wide Web ... Now even my cat has its own page.
Bill Clinton, 1996

HOME PAGE

On a website, the page that acts as a front door to everything else. Such home pages typically provide a comprehensive index of the site's content and the NAVIGATION tools needed to move around it. Usually, the website's main address is also the home page address.

For web surfers, the home page is the first page that appears when they start their BROWSER, often a PORTAL or other site preset by their ISP or browser manufacturer. Pressing the "Home" button in the browser returns a user to this page. Any other site can be specified as the default browser home page; a SEARCH ENGINE, for example, or a different portal.

HOST

Broadly, any computer acting as a repository for information, data or services that can be accessed by another computer across a NETWORK. On the Internet the meaning is more specific, encompassing any computer that has its own IP ADDRESS and full two-way access to other NODES on the network.

HOTWIRED

A website originally established by *Wired* magazine, now owned and run by LYCOS. Hotwired is best known for its invention of the BANNER advertisement.

HTCPCP

Hypertext Coffee Pot Control Protocol (see RFC).

HTML

Hypertext Mark-up Language, used to create documents and links on the WORLD WIDE WEB. HTML is a simple, text-based set of instructions, known as TAGS, which describe how the elements of a web page should be laid out and how they connect to other documents or programs. Much of the web's success can be attributed to the accessibility and simplicity of this language, which anyone with a text editor and a simple reference guide can write. Despite (or perhaps because of) this simplicity, writing reams of HTML code is dull work, and many programs now exist to automate the process.

Unlike real programming languages such as C++ or JAVA, which need to be compiled for a specific OPERATING SYSTEM, HTML is – in theory, at least – interpreted by all browsers in the same way, regardless of their manufacturer or the type of computer they run on. HTML standards (including the latest, version 4) are administered by the W3C, which works hard to ensure that they are widely adopted. But the BROWSER manufacturers have not been co-operative in enforcing these standards. Both MICROSOFT and NETSCAPE have hijacked the HTML specification and made their own incompatible additions to it, with the result that code written for INTERNET EXPLORER may look completely different (or not work at all) in NAVIGATOR, and vice versa. This represents a problem for site developers, who must consider writing at least two versions of their pages to ensure that everyone can read them properly.

HTTP

Hypertext Transfer Protocol, the PROTOCOL used to transfer web pages between a web SERVER and a BROWSER. HTTP was created at CERN by Tim Berners-Lee and his team as part of the development of the WORLD WIDE WEB.

HYPERLINK

See LINK.

HYPERTEXT

Text that can be read in a non-linear fashion, by following a series of links between related sections of material. Typical applications for hypertext include reference works such as encyclopedias or dictionaries, where interesting or useful explanations of highlighted words in the text can be reached by clicking on them with a mouse. Many computer help systems use hypertext to guide users and illustrate common procedures; and hypertext is slowly creeping into our culture in the form of novels and even video installations.

By far the biggest hypertext application is the WORLD WIDE WEB, which uses its HTML and HTTP technologies to link together hundreds of millions of individual pages. (Strictly speaking, the web is a hypermedia system, as it incorporates graphics, video and audio into the text framework.) The web makes something of a mockery of the many lofty hypertext theories that have been propounded over the years, most of which want to impose a predetermined structure and format on hypertext documents. It simply works, despite the lack of consistent guiding principles among its builders.

The term hypertext was coined by Ted Nelson

in the 1960s to describe his XANADU system. But hypertext-like systems had been described before, most presciently by Vannevar Bush in 1945, whose theoretical microfilm-based "memex" device included a number of features for linking together information recorded on microfilm.

ICANN

The Internet Corporation for Assigned Names and Numbers, a private non-profit organisation responsible for managing the systems and PROTOCOLS that keep the Internet running. In particular, ICANN is responsible for allocating IP ADDRESSES, managing the DOMAIN NAME SYSTEM and taking over other tasks currently under US government contract to other agencies, such as the Internet Assigned Names Authority (IANA). ICANN was formed in 1998 to help bring an independent, international focus to the management of the Internet.

ICQ

Messaging software that lets people communicate electronically in real time; in effect, a CHAT program. ICQ (a contraction of I Seek You) has attracted millions of users, who can not only chat but also send files and URLS, play games and even communicate by video, either individually or as part of a group. This rapidly growing COMMUNITY inevitably attracted the attention of AOL, to which the program's developer Mirabilis was sold in 1998.

IETF

The Internet Engineering Task Force, a self-organised group which shepherds the development of new technical standards for the Internet. Its brief includes identifying technical problems, proposing and specifying the development of solutions to these problems and providing a forum for the exchange of information within the Internet COMMUNITY. Despite the fact that the IETF is not a traditional standards organisation – its ad hoc structure and open-to-all policy would make the leaders of most analogous organisations shudder – it produces many specifications that become Internet standards. Its main unit of currency is the RFC (Request For Comments), a document that details a new technological solution to a particular problem. Comments from relevant experts then guide the development of that technology. One of the

IETF's stipulations for any proposal is that the standard in question must actually exist, preferably in prototype. This is one of the reasons for the Internet's rapid technical progress.

We reject kings, presidents and voting. We believe in rough consensus and running code.
Seen on an IETF T-shirt

IMAGE
A picture stored in electronic form. Images that appear on web pages are generally stored in one of the few formats that can be understood by a web BROWSER: GIF, JPEG or PNG. All of these formats use COMPRESSION techniques to reduce the size of the image files and thus speed up DOWNLOAD times.

IMAGE MAP
A clickable image used to help users navigate around and between websites. An image map is divided into several different hotspot areas, each of which is linked to another destination. A CLICK with the mouse on one of these hotspots will take the user to the URL associated with it.

IMAP
Internet Message Access Protocol, a standard way of retrieving E-MAIL from a mail SERVER. The main advantage of IMAP over older protocols such as POP3 is that users can manipulate remote mailboxes as if they were on a local machine. This makes it much easier for recipients to specify how they receive their e-mail. They can, for example, view just the subject and sender of an e-mail before deciding whether to download it, or specify that only messages meeting certain criteria should be viewed. IMAP allows the creation and manipulation of folders on the server rather than on a local hard disk, making it easier and more convenient to organise e-mail. Another advantage is that mail stays on IMAP servers until a user deletes it. POP mail, in contrast, is usually deleted

as soon as it is delivered, making it impossible to read from a different machine at a later date.

IMPRESSION

A single instance of the display of a specific web page or, more commonly, a BANNER advertisement. Impressions are measured by the number of requests from BROWSERS for particular banners, as counted by specialised ad counters. Advertisers pay for a certain number of impressions, rather than a number of HITS.

INCREASING RETURNS

The idea that the more dominant a company becomes, the bigger its future advantage over competitors will be. It is especially relevant to the high-tech industry, where the winner of one technological race is likely to start the next with an advantage. The increasing returns concept formed the basis of the original antitrust suit in the United States against MICROSOFT, whose dominance in the OPERATING SYSTEM market was said by its competitors to give an unfair advantage in the emerging BROWSER market. This, in turn, would give it excessive leverage in future areas of development and provide a high barrier to the entry of new competitors.

INFOMEDIARY

An electronic intermediary that helps buyers and sellers do business on the Internet, usually by providing unique or exclusive information and services. There are many examples of infomediaries, the best-known being consumer-driven websites such as lastminute.com and EBAY. Both of these bring buyers and sellers together in ways not practical before the advent of public electronic networks by consolidating geographically isolated customers and suppliers. But the real future for infomediaries is in BUSINESS-TO-BUSINESS transactions, where the ability to provide up-to-the-minute pricing information, supply goods at rock-bottom prices or merely host a conveniently neutral dealing platform will give Internet-based businesses a huge advantage over their real-world equivalents. For an interesting contrast, and an example of the difficulty of making predictions on Internet trends, see also DISINTERMEDIATION.

INFONESIA

The inability to remember where you came across a particular piece of information. This irritating ailment is becoming much more prevalent as the number of digital information sources in people's lives increases, and most infonesiacs are long-term users of E-MAIL, NEWSGROUPS and MAILING LISTS. A related condition, internesia, is common among avid web surfers and CYBRARIANS.

INFORMATION APPLIANCE

A device that connects to a digital network or broadcast service for the purpose of gathering or distributing information. After the telephone, the Internet-connected PC is the most common and useful information appliance. In the business world, this is not likely to change in the near future. As Oracle's well-meaning but badly conceived NETWORK COMPUTER showed, people still want powerful, multipurpose machines that can do a wide variety of jobs. But PCs are less attractive to consumers (the biggest market for information appliances) as they are still expensive and complex by the standards of household goods. They are also bulky, which reduces their value as general-purpose information-gathering devices. These facts are driving the development of a vast range of new devices to help people connect to information resources with a minimal investment of time, effort and money. Examples include personal digital assistants (PDAs) capable of making wireless connections to the Internet and digital mobile phones embedded in wristwatches.

INTERLACED

Describes a characteristic of a graphic IMAGE, which enables alternating rows of the image to be displayed in separate passes as it downloads. A fuzzy but complete version of the image thus appears quickly in the BROWSER and gets progressively sharper as the details are filled in. The GIF files used on many web pages are usually interlaced. A similar technique is used to improve the resolution of computer monitors.

INTERNET EXPLORER
Software for browsing the WORLD WIDE WEB developed by MICROSOFT (see BROWSER).

INTERNET OPEN TRADING PROTOCOL
A PROTOCOL designed to standardise electronic payment transactions on the Internet. As anyone who has bought things from more than one website will testify, most traders and retailers on the Internet use their own complex and incompatible systems for making financial transactions, agreeing only on the ENCRYPTION standards that protect their details from prying eyes. The Internet Open Trading Protocol (IOTP) tries to recreate some of the accepted practices that govern real-world buying and selling, complete with subtleties such as the way a transaction is conducted, the presentation of offers and the delivery and receipt of goods. Theoretically, IOTP should make life much easier for consumers, who will be able to use a consistent interface for buying and ordering goods and services, as well as for merchants and banks, who will have more consistent ways of collecting and processing payments. In practice, it is likely to be a long time before it is widely used. Bodies implementing new Internet standards do not always share users' views about consistency and ease of use, and many good ideas like this (the Open Profiling Standard, OPS, for example) have yet to be usefully implemented anywhere.

INTERNET SOCIETY
An international non-profit organisation which guides the development of the Internet. Formed in 1992, the Internet Society is the organisational home of the bodies that govern technical Internet standards, including the Internet Engineering Task Force (IETF) and the Internet Architecture Board (IAB).

INTERNET TELEPHONY

Techniques for transmitting voice and fax over the
Internet. There are two ways of making telephone
calls across the Internet. The first, which relies on
the use of a PC, is especially attractive because it is
essentially free, regardless of distance. The only
charge is for the local call between the PC and an
ISP – the same cost as any other dial-up Internet
connection used for browsing the web or sending
E-MAIL. Special hardware and software compress
and convert the sound of a voice (or a fax
machine) into a BINARY FILE, which is then broken
up into PACKETS just as any other message would
be. The PC at the recipient's end of the call then
converts the packets back into an audible voice
signal.

There are several problems with this sort of
communication. Perhaps the biggest is that recipients of PC-to-PC phone calls must not only have
their own IP ADDRESS but must also be using the
same hardware and software combination as the
person making the call, as the many products on
the market are not yet generally interoperable.
Also the quality of service (QOS) is far from perfect
because of the inherent difficulties in managing
time lags across the Internet and reassembling
packets in the right order. Once these problems
are resolved, this kind of Internet telephony will
be a realistic option for everyone. At present,
however, its use is restricted to private, managed
networks in corporate environments, where
callers can be sure that the relevant hardware and
software is installed on every recipient's PC and
QOS is easier to ensure.

The second way of using the Internet to make
phone calls simply uses a normal telephone.
Instead of the call being routed all the way on
public telephone networks it is converted into IP
PACKETS and then routed via the Internet. At the
other end, the digitised voice is converted back
again by a local server. Although this kind of call
still suffers from the same packet reassembly
problems, it gets over the compatibility issue –
sender and receiver need only standard telephone

equipment. The inevitable sting in the tail is that this requires co-operation from the telephone companies, which have so far been reluctant to install the required IP-TO-PSTN GATEWAYS needed to connect the public networks to the Internet. Limited services are available in some countries, including the United States.

INTERNET2

An experimental high-speed NETWORK. Formed in 1996 by a consortium of American universities, Internet2 was designed as a testbed for new networking technologies and applications, especially those needing very high speeds. Despite its name, it is not a replacement for the existing Internet; rather, its operators hope that research and developments stemming from Internet2 will find their way on to the mainstream Internet as higher BANDWIDTH and better technology becomes available. Current areas of research on Internet2 include delivery of educational and health services, digital video, IP v6 and MULTICASTING. Over 160 universities, many of which are connected to other high-speed networks such as VBNS, are now members of Internet2.

INTERNET TIME

Time taken to get things done in the fast-moving Internet environment. Not a clearly-defined fraction of standard linear timescales, but nonetheless a measure of the fact that things happen faster on the Internet than in the real world. This transformative effect is especially apparent in the software and hardware industries, where an already rapid rate of change has been greatly accelerated by extreme competition and massive demand for new products and services.

The term is also used to describe a new, standardised global time measurement system proposed by Swatch, a Swiss watch manufacturer, which divides the day into 1,000 units called beats. Interest in this idea has so far been limited.

INTERNIC

Until recently, the American organisation responsible for registering and maintaining top-level DOMAIN names, in conjunction with NETWORK SOLUTIONS. Since 1998 the registration process has been open to competition, with ICANN assuming responsibility for accreditation and the appointment of new registrars.

INTERSTITIAL PAGE

A page inserted into the structure of a website that displays an advertisement or other form of promotion. When visitors click on a link, the interstitial page pops up for a few seconds before taking them to the page they intended to view. Some sites force users to endure interstitial pages before the home page loads, either for creative effect or simply to maximise exposure to an advertisement, which can be sold much more expensively than a typical BANNER. Poor site design has occasionally resulted in interstitial pages leading directly on to other interstitial pages, locking site visitors into a perpetual loop of advertisements.

INTRANET

A NETWORK based on the same technical standards as the Internet, but designed for use within a single organisation. Intranets are rapidly replacing proprietary networks in companies because they are generally simpler and cheaper to administer. Indeed, it is possible to build an intranet without paying for any software at all by running free E-MAIL, BROWSERS and web SERVERS on top of the TCP/IP software supplied with all major OPERATING SYSTEMS. In practice, most organisations use commercial software from networking companies such as NOVELL to build and administer their networks. A 1998 survey of telecoms managers by IDC, a research company, found that over 60% of large British companies were planning to install an intranet by the end of that year. In the United States, companies spent an estimated $10.9 billion on Intranet development in the same year.

Intranets are extremely flexible, and are used to

create everything from simple employee directories (much cheaper than printing 1,000 copies) to complex DATABASE and GROUPWARE applications. The open technology on which they are based makes intranets much easier to customise than expensive proprietary products like Lotus NOTES, which has forced manufacturers of such products to re-engineer their software in recent years. Unfortunately, it also makes them more open to attack from the outside, so intranets must be carefully protected by a FIREWALL, or at the very least a solid security policy. This is particularly important once the logical leap to an EXTRANET is made.

IP
Internet Protocol (see TCP/IP).

IP ADDRESS
The address of a particular computer on the Internet, used to identify it uniquely for communications purposes. Every computer that sends or receives information on the Internet must have an IP address, expressed as a 32-BIT number, which is attached to every message that is sent. Thus the recipient of any message has a return address to which it can reply if necessary. This is especially important on the web, where a SERVER must know exactly where to send back a requested page.

According to the current version of the IP PROTOCOL, version 4, the number itself is arranged in four groups of up to three numbers and has two parts: one identifies the network on which a machine resides and the other is for the machine itself. Each group is represented by a number between 0 and 255, giving numbers like 207.87.8.50. These numbers are translated into the alphabetic names associated with them (www.economist.com in the above example) by a NAME SERVER.

Although the number of individual addresses supported by this system is huge, many numbers are reserved for special purposes and are not available for use by companies or individuals. The incredible growth of the Internet has rapidly depleted the available numbers, especially those designated for use with small networks (known as Class C addresses). Enter IP version 6, already implemented in some OPERATING SYSTEMS, which will use 128-bit numbers. This new system, sometimes known as IPng (for "new generation"), theoretically enables 340,282,366,920,938,463,463,374, 607,431,768,211,456 possible addresses; or 665, 570,793,348,866,943,898,599 for each square metre of the Earth. This should be enough for even the most information-hungry economy.

IPO

Initial Public Offering, a term for the first sale of publicly tradeable shares by a company that has previously been privately owned, otherwise known as going public. IPOS are a crucial stage in a company's evolution, as they generate substantial income from the sale of the initial batch of shares and, more importantly, establish the company's credentials with the trading community. Internet companies have become famous for the success of their IPOS, which have generated fortunes for the owners of CISCO, EBAY, NETSCAPE, YAHOO and hundreds of others. In 2000 the IPO for AT&T's wireless division raised over $10 billion on the first day's trading, an American record for any company. But in early 2000 the markets demonstrated their unpredictability as high-tech stocks took a dive not long after successful IPOS of such companies as Lastminute.com in the UK, which led to ALTAVISTA and others delaying their IPOS.

IRC

Internet Relay Chat, a popular way of communicating on the Internet. Using special CHAT software, users connect to one of many chat servers around the world. Each SERVER contains a number of chat areas, called channels, which are in theory devoted to a particular subject; #cricket, for example, should be about cricket. Once connected to a channel, anything you type is instantly readable by anyone else on the channel.

IRC attracts an enormous number of enthusiasts

and, unsurprisingly, more than its fair share of eccentrics. Many an IRC NEWBIE finds its arcane commands and lively participants a little harsh when compared with the cosiness of an ONLINE SERVICE providers' chat rooms. Nonetheless, IRC has been used to transmit news from some otherwise inaccessible places; inside the Russian parliament building while it was being shelled in 1993, for example.

IRL

In Real Life, commonly used in CHAT rooms and NEWSGROUPS. A typical comment is "So what do you look like IRL?", often accompanied by a SMILEY.

ISDN

Integrated Services Digital Network. Long touted as the next generation of high-BANDWIDTH digital communications services, ISDN is still the most widely available alternative to the plain old telephone system (POTS) as a means of connecting to the Internet.

As its name suggests, an ISDN line integrates data and voice calls, so that it is possible to make phone calls while connected to the Internet or other services. For most users, however, the higher bandwidth is the real attraction. The standard ISDN connection is called the basic rate interface (BRI) and consists of three data channels: two B (bearer) channels of 64K each which carry the data, and a 16K D (delta) channel for transmitting calling information. Thus a BRI line can transmit data at 128K BITS per second, about three times the speed of a POTS connection. Some users opt for the primary rate interface (PRI), which in Europe consists of 30 B channels and one D channel.

Phone companies typically charge considerably more for ISDN than POTS, despite the fact that it is often cheaper for them to support. It also requires a special piece of equipment, called a terminal adapter, to connect a PC to ISDN, adding more cost to the package. These factors, and some poor marketing, have held back ISDN's progress in the UK, although it is popular in the United States and elsewhere in Europe. New technologies such as ADSL will gradually supersede ISDN.

ISP

Internet Service Provider, a company that provides direct connections to the Internet. ISPs form the GATEWAY between the public telephone network and the Internet itself, and make it possible for anyone with a computer and a MODEM to gain access to a full set of Internet services. All ISPs supply subscribers with an E-MAIL address. Most also provide web-hosting facilities, allowing anyone with a text-editing program and a smattering of HTML knowledge to build their own website.

Few kinds of companies have been forced to evolve as fast as ISPs. Since their advent in the early 1990s they have endured massive increases in the numbers of users, several changes of business model, legal and ethical tests over PORNOGRAPHY and libel issues, and some drastic changes in technology. Many have not survived this onslaught, and in its characteristically democratic way the Internet has made life hard for service providers big and small. Even MICROSOFT, the world's richest company, has found the ISP business tough going. Nonetheless, the number of companies providing Internet access worldwide continues to grow in line with the demand – a demand so fierce that some surprising companies have gone into the ISP business with the expectation of making money. Tesco, a British supermarket chain, is a good example.

In this kind of market, differentiating yourself from a competitor is a difficult job. BANDWIDTH and consistency of service, the two biggest issues for subscribers, have levelled out across ISPs, and it took FREESERVE's move to a free access model to stir things up in the British market. Predictably, many others followed the company's example, and another shake-out seems sure to follow.

JANET

ACRONYM for Joint Academic Network, a high-speed UK BACKBONE connecting several hundred academic and educational institutions. Janet and its fibre-based BROADBAND cousin SuperJanet are part of the global Internet.

JAVA

A programming language created by SUN MICROSYSTEMS which began life as a way to connect intelligent devices in the home. It has since evolved into a sprawling set of NETWORK software technologies that allow information to be transmitted and shared by a wide variety of devices. Java has generated enthusiasm bordering on religious mania in the software development community, and many observers have predicted that it will in time break Microsoft's stranglehold on the computer desktop.

From a programmer's viewpoint, Java is easier, faster to use and more elegant than languages such as C++. It can still be used for large-scale projects, and several commercial software vendors have released Java-only versions of their business and graphics software applications. But Java's greatest promise is that software programs written in it will run on any computer, regardless of the OPERATING SYSTEM or processor it uses. Such PORTABILITY is achieved by way of a VIRTUAL MACHINE (VM), a piece of software specific to a particular operating system that interprets the BYTECODE in a Java program and translates it for use in the local environment. This "write once, run anywhere" property is immensely attractive to software developers, who have previously been burdened by the necessity of writing separate versions of their programs for each PLATFORM or operating system: one for WINDOWS, one for WINDOWS NT, one for Macintoshes, and so on.

A second benefit of Java is security. Virtual machines insulate Java programs from the HOST machine's hardware and software, and thus limit their ability to damage the system. This is often cited as one of Java's main advantages over MICROSOFT'S ACTIVEX technology, which imposes no such limitations and whose potential dangers have been widely publicised.

These two attributes have done much to popularise Java in the developer community. But its third characteristic, modularity, is arguably the most important. Many people associate Java only with APPLETS and the WORLD WIDE WEB, but its reach is far broader. Java is a fully OBJECT-ORIENTED language, well-suited to the creation of components, each with their own specific functions, that can communicate locally or across networks, on servers and in clients. Sun's complete list of Java-related products and technologies contains over 50 specifications that extend Java's capabilities, including the JAVABEANS component technology, PersonalJava, EmbeddedJava, Java Servlets and JINI.

Such far-reaching usefulness sounds too good to be true, and in some ways it is. The missionary zeal with which Java's evangelists promote it conceals some awkward truths that seriously reduce Java's chances of toppling Windows from its throne. One common complaint is that Java virtual machines are still slow, which frustrates many web users anxiously waiting for something to happen on their screens (an ironic exception is the VM written by Microsoft, which turns out to be considerably faster than its competitors). More importantly, the "write once, run anywhere" promise has turned out to be misleading and irrelevant, as developers have discovered the need to use specific features of operating systems to make their products really useful. This in turn has compromised Java's much-vaunted security model.

These failings have led to some bitter disputes between Sun and Microsoft, which has produced a range of supposedly Java-compliant products that, it claims, improve on Sun's lowest-common-denominator originals. Sun accused Microsoft of infringing its Java licence by leaving out key Java features from some products – an accusation supported by an American judge in 1998.

JavaBeans

A set of OBJECT-ORIENTED programming tools

created by SUN MICROSYSTEMS, based on the JAVA programming language. JavaBeans is used to create small component programs, called beans, that perform specific functions; an interest-rate calculator, for example, or a simple drawing program. Beans have some basic communication skills and can talk to each other to find out if and how they can work together. This makes them extremely flexible and able to work in lots of places; an interest-rate calculator could be used in a web page on a building society's INTRANET and as part of a standalone spreadsheet program designed for more general use. (See COM.)

JAVASCRIPT

A programming language designed to enhance the capabilities of web pages. The brainchild of NETSCAPE, Javascript is a relative of C++ but is designed for completely different tasks and is much easier to learn. It should not be confused with JAVA. Its main purpose is to help a web BROWSER do things that are beyond the scope of pure HTML, such as popping up special windows in response to mouse clicks or displaying messages in its status bar.

Many Javascript applications on the web are decidedly trivial, but it has some powerful features and forms a central part of DHTML. Javascript might check a web form for completeness before returning it to the SERVER, or change the colour of text blocks when the mouse pointer passes over them. Most browsers now support Javascript, and MICROSOFT has even copied the idea with the rather less popular Jscript. One problem with Javascript (and, indeed, Java) is that not all browsers like it; code that NAVIGATOR runs well can easily crash INTERNET EXPLORER, and vice versa.

JINI

A way to connect hardware devices on a NETWORK intelligently, irrespective of their make or type. When a device is added to a Jini-based network, it posts a list of its resources and capabilities to a central DATABASE used by every other device on the network. When something else comes along that wants to use those services, the instructions for how to do so are already contained in the database. Thus a Jini-enabled printer can be used by all the PCs, wireless PDAs and even televisions on a particular network, without the need for each to have special driver software or even the same OPERATING SYSTEM.

Jini is the invention of SUN MICROSYSTEMS, and is based on its JAVA technology. Sun's ambitions for its latest offspring are characteristically ambitious. Jini's various champions have described a gigantic future global computer network, in which everything understands everything else and technology is freed from the tyranny of large, monopolistic suppliers of operating systems (especially those owned by people called Gates). Even though they have heard this sort of thing before, several manufacturers have been testing devices that will help fulfil this Utopian vision. The first machines are expected to go on sale some time in 2000.

JPEG
A type of compressed IMAGE file, based on a specification by the Joint Picture Experts Group. JPEG-encoded images (often known simply as JPGs) are often used on websites because of the comparatively small size of their files. (See also MPEG.)

JUNK E-MAIL
See SPAM.

JUST-IN-TIME COMPILER
A program that turns JAVA BYTECODE into processor-specific executable software. Just-in-time (JIT) compilers can help overcome the sluggish performance of a web BROWSER'S VIRTUAL MACHINE, which runs bytecode one instruction at a time. If the code in which a Java APPLET is written is translated into native code that the computer understands, the underlying program can often be run much faster. JIT compilers are supplied with virtual machines from many companies, including SUN, MICROSOFT, NETSCAPE and IBM.

K

Abbreviation for kilo-, used to denote a multiplier of a thousand. So a 28.8K modem receives data at 28,800 bits per second, and the Motorola 68000 chip found in older Apple computers is sometimes referred to as the 68K.

KBPS

Thousands of BITS, or kilobits, per second (see MBPS).

KEY

A string of data used to decode an encrypted message. The length of the key, usually quoted in BITS, determines how secure the message is. (See ENCRYPTION.)

KEYWORD

An index entry in a DATABASE that identifies a document or record. Keyword searches form the basis of operation of SEARCH ENGINES such as ALTAVISTA, which search web pages for unique words and index them accordingly. The simplicity of this approach belies the difficulty of obtaining useful results from databases of several million documents, and most search engines use additional criteria to determine the relevance of a particular keyword's occurrence.

Some search engines have attracted controversy by selling keywords to advertisers and ranking searches for these words preferentially. Many others associate keywords with particular advertisements, so that a search for "computer" will display a computer vendor's BANNER at the top of the search results page. PORNOGRAPHY sites have taken particular advantage of this feature, to the displeasure of many web users confronted with graphic advertisements following innocent searches, especially for words describing parts of the body.

KEY ESCROW

A scheme whereby anyone using PUBLIC KEY CRYPTOGRAPHY must deposit a copy of their key with a designated agency or TRUSTED THIRD PARTY. When security agencies wish to eavesdrop on encrypted conversations or read encrypted files, a warrant of some sort would allow them to retrieve the key from its escrow. Unsurprisingly, there has been worldwide opposition to key escrow schemes by privacy campaigners. (See ENCRYPTION.)

KILLER APP

A piece of software that creates the market for a promising technology. The best-known example of a killer app is the spreadsheet, first in the shape of Visicalc and then Lotus 1-2-3. The latter drove the early market for IBM PCs by offering number-crunching facilities for which every business could see an immediate use. Most successful computer technologies have a killer app behind them, often a generic one. The most obvious example from the 1990s is E-MAIL, undoubtedly the application that has attracted millions of businesses and consumers to the wider Internet.

The US Postal Service delivered 101 billion pieces of paper mail in 1998. Estimates for e-mail messages sent in the same year range from 618 billion to 4 trillion.

LAN

See LOCAL AREA NETWORK

LATENCY

Broadly, a term used to describe a delay in transmitting data between two computers. Latency is the time taken to transfer a PACKET of information from one point to another, and is often cited as one of the reasons for the sluggish performance of Internet connections.

Many factors influence the latency of a NETWORK connection, including the nature of the medium (cable, fibre, and so on), the number of ROUTERS, the efficiency of a MODEM or network card and, ultimately, the speed of light. Although the delays introduced by each of these are measured in milliseconds, they add up to a significant total when applied to every packet of data sent across the network. This is one of the reasons that modes of communication that rely on sending a large number of messages back and forth, such as videoconferencing and ONLINE GAMING, are susceptible to latency problems.

LDAP

Lightweight Directory Access Protocol, a PROTOCOL which helps find people, computers and other resources on a NETWORK. Designed to work with existing address-book standards such as X.500 and improve compatibility between widely differing systems, the LDAP standard was adopted by the IETF in 1997 and now forms the basis of many white-page directories on the web. It has also been incorporated directly into some software programs and OPERATING SYSTEMS, making it possible to find E-MAIL addresses without visiting a directory site.

LEASED LINE

A communications line that is rented for private use. Leased lines, sometimes known as dedicated lines, have a number of benefits for companies sending or receiving large amounts of data. The biggest is that the fixed BANDWIDTH of the line (which can vary from POTS speed to high-speed fibre or satellite rates, depending on how much you are prepared to pay) is not shared with anyone else, thus guaranteeing a particular level of service. This contrasts with FRAME RELAY connections, which share lines with other users.

LINK

A connection between two HYPERTEXT objects, used to help people navigate on the WORLD WIDE WEB. Generally, a link takes the form of a highlighted word, phrase or graphic IMAGE on a web page. Clicking on a link then displays the object to which the link points, known as the target, which can be a different web page, a marked location further down the same web page or even a program on an FTP site. For all their simplicity, hypertext links are the key to the web's power. As well as forming its skeleton, they are an increasingly useful measure of the relevance of websites. Some SEARCH ENGINES, notably Google, rate the importance of pages on the basis of the number of links to them from elsewhere.

LINKROT

A gradual process whereby links from web pages to other pages or sites become unusable, usually resulting in a 404 NOT FOUND message. Linkrot is generally caused by sites reorganising their structure and moving or deleting pages in the process, or by the closure of a site. Despite the availability of many site management tools that track and maintain links, some surveys show that almost one in four web pages contains bad links.

LINUX

A powerful, freely available computer OPERATING SYSTEM. Linux was created by Linus Torvalds, a Finnish student, as a result of his frustration with commercial operating systems such as MICROSOFT WINDOWS and Apple's MacOs. Originally based on a slimmed-down version of the UNIX operating system, called Minix, Torvalds's creation has become an impressive and highly capable operating system in its own right, and now represents a real threat to the Microsoft WINDOWS NT hegemony.

Although Linux was originally the work of Torvalds, the system has evolved from the efforts of hundreds of programmers working collaboratively and philanthropically in the OPEN SOURCE spirit. The heart of the system is still written and maintained by Torvalds and a handful of generals, who regularly add new features and tweak old ones. Additions to the system, such as drivers for printers and scanners, are written and tested by members of the far-flung Linux community, working and communicating through a number of dedicated NEWSGROUPS. Through this real-world testing and development, Linux has achieved a degree of stability and usefulness that matches or even exceeds that of commercial operating systems.

Many ISPS now use Linux as the basis for their services in preference to Windows NT or Unix, and it has gained a solid reputation in some vertical markets such as advanced graphics and IMAGE processing. Many of the effects for the film "Titanic" were created on Linux machines. It is also the operating system of choice for many web SERVERS because of its robustness and its ability to handle hundreds or thousands of simultaneous users, and over 1m websites now run on it. Leading industry figures such as Oracle's Larry Ellison have advocated Linux as a real alternative to Windows. Slowly but surely Linux is gaining ground in the business community, its opportunity increased by the late delivery of Microsoft's WINDOWS 2000 and the availability of powerful business applications, from Oracle, Corel and many others, which are written for Linux.

Critics of Linux cite its independence as a major problem for corporate users needing guaranteed technical support and managed upgrades for business-critical systems. Many versions lack a graphical user interface and are considered hard to install and configure. But fully supported commercial versions with GUI front-ends are now widely available from companies such as Red Hat Software, and because the Linux SOURCE CODE is freely available organisations with sufficient resources can build custom versions to meet specific business needs. Whether Linux succeeds or fails in the business world depends largely on the continued and expanding support of third parties such as Red Hat, and the willingness of companies to commit to its installation and use on a large scale.

LINX

Stands for the London Internet Exchange, a neutral interconnection point for many British ISPs and the largest IXP (point of network interconnection) in Europe, acting as a central hub where data can be moved quickly between carriers and BACK-BONES. LINX, which is housed in London's TELE-HOUSE, is designed to speed traffic between ISPs by providing a direct link between them at a single central point. The flaw in this apparently good idea became abundantly clear in 1997, when a power surge at Telehouse caused much of the UK's Internet to disappear for 10 minutes. Several other IXPs have since appeared, including MANAP in Manchester and SCOTIX in Scotland, with the aim of spreading the risk of future NETWORK failures.

LIST SERVER

A program that manages the distribution of electronic newsletters and other messages to a MAILING LIST's subscribers. List servers respond to E-MAIL requests, automatically adding or removing subscribers to a list and arranging for all future messages to be sent to them. Nearly all aspects of list server administration can be handled by e-mail, making them easy to operate remotely. Two popular list servers are LISTSERV and MAJORDOMO.

LISTSERV

A popular LIST SERVER (see also MAJORDOMO).

LOCAL AREA NETWORK

A NETWORK that links nearby computers to one another. A local area network (LAN) is usually used to connect computers in the same room or on the same floor of a building, and often forms part of a much bigger corporate network. Most LANS are based on one or more FILE SERVERS, which hold centralised applications and files that can be accessed from the network's constituent workstations. Most LANS use either the Ethernet or Token Ring methods of managing information flow across the network, alongside network OPERATING SYSTEMS such as NETWARE or WINDOWS NT, which manage users and network resources. Increasingly, LANS use standard Internet PROTOCOLS such as TCP/IP for transmitting data rather than proprietary ones, and thus form the underlying skeleton for an INTRANET.

LOCAL LOOP

The link between a customer's telephone socket and the nearest telephone switch. Each loop is dedicated to a single customer. Most existing links were designed for voice transmission using analog devices, rather than modern digital equipment, and still consist of a pair of copper wires. Local loops are the most unpredictable parts of the telephone system, as the wires may be old and damaged. This is one potential barrier to the widescale implementation of new digital technologies such as ADSL, which are partially dependent on the quality of the local loop cables.

LOGIN

A user validation process imposed by many computer systems before they can be used. A successful login generally depends on a user entering a valid name and a PASSWORD before access to the computer's resources is granted, although some OPERATING SYSTEMS demand extra steps. WINDOWS NT, for example, requires users to press the Control, Alt and Delete keys simultaneously, as protection against TROJAN HORSE programs designed to break system security. May also be referred to as logon.

LURKER

Someone who hovers in the background in CHAT

rooms and NEWSGROUPS without contributing to the discussion; effectively, an electronic voyeur. Lurking is generally regarded as a harmless pastime, especially among NEWBIES and the terminally shy. The process of breaking silence and contributing to a discussion for the first time is called delurking.

LYCOS

One of the first SEARCH ENGINES. Launched in 1995 with technology developed at Carnegie Mellon University, Lycos was named after the wolf spider family, the *Lycosidae*. In 1996 Lycos's IPO made it the youngest company to go public in the history of the NASDAQ stock exchange. The company has diversified widely since its inception, acquiring several web communities such as Tripod and Angelfire, as well as E-MAIL company MailCity, the Hotbot search engine and the HOTWIRED network. In May 2000 the company announced a $12 billion merger deal with Terra Networks, a spin-off of Spanish telecoms giant Telefonica, in a move that will place it among the few truly global Internet companies and a potential competitor to the newly formed AOL Time Warner.

MAE

Metropolitan Area Exchange, a centre in the United States for switching traffic between ISPs. There are two major exchanges: MAE-East in Washington, DC, which connects ISPs in the eastern United States with European ISPs; and MAE-West in San José, which connects ISPs in Silicon Valley. There are smaller tier 2 MAEs throughout the United States. Like LINX, the MAE networks allow digital traffic between ISPs to travel quickly. In essence, each is a giant LOCAL AREA NETWORK switch to which ISPs connect their ROUTERS. One complicated and sometimes contentious feature of the MAE set-up is that ISPs must negotiate between themselves over which carries whose traffic.

MAILING LIST

An E-MAIL distribution list, used to circulate requested information or group discussions. Mailing lists rival NEWSGROUPS in their diversity, and are used for everything from the simple dissemination of product information to heated discussions of the finer points of non-ferrous metal welding.

There are two types of mailing lists.

- Closed lists are maintained by an individual or organisation and send information one way only. Such lists are used to distribute, say, daily newsletters or regular weather updates to a subscriber list. Many websites and computer vendors use mailing lists to keep customers up to date on improvements to services or software and hardware.
- Open lists allow subscribers to contribute to discussions by replying to messages as they arrive. Each reply is then distributed to everyone else on the list. Most open lists are unmoderated, which means that everyone on the list gets every message as soon as it is posted. On big mailing lists, this generates an enormous amount of e-mail traffic, much of which is irrelevant or off-topic. Moderated lists are generally more satisfactory, as the moderators eliminate irrelevant or repetitive

messages and generally improve the flow of discussion.

Anyone with access to an Internet SERVER can set up a mailing list (hence the vast number of lists in circulation) using server software such as LISTSERV or MAJORDOMO.

MAJORDOMO

Software used to manage a MAILING LIST. Unlike LISTSERV systems, which all interconnect with each other and provide access to a global list of lists, Majordomo hosts are independent, standalone entities.

MBPS

Millions of BITS per second or megabits per second, generally used as a measure of BANDWIDTH. Currently, only the fastest NETWORK connections, such as ADSL or T1 lines, can carry data in multiple millions of bits per second. A standard analog MODEM of the sort widely used for a dial-up Internet connection is capable of speeds measured in tens of thousands of bits per second.

MBONE

Multicast Backbone, a high-speed Internet BACKBONE designed for sending large files such as video segments to multiple users. Unlike normal Internet transmissions, which rely on the one-to-one capabilities of the IP PROTOCOL, Mbone transmissions allow material such as live concert footage or radio broadcasts to be sent to thousands of people simultaneously. Instead of sending a copy of the file to everybody, the multicast protocol sends out a single file which copies itself only when necessary. So if 50 people at economist.com request a copy of a 20-MEGABYTE news broadcast from an American server, just one copy of the file is sent and duplicated once it arrives at the economist.com NETWORK. This greatly reduces the amount of traffic travelling across the Internet, as only 20 megabytes of information needs to be transmitted instead of 1 gigabyte. At the same time it increases demands on the recipient's system hardware.

M-COMMERCE
Mobile commerce, widely predicted to be the next wave of E-COMMERCE. M-commerce, sometimes known as m-business, encapsulates any kind of information transfer or transaction that can be initiated from a mobile phone or other portable information appliance device. Commonly cited examples include booking of services such as flights or other tickets, personal banking and share trades. Currently, the biggest market for m-commerce services is in Europe, where mobile phone penetration is extremely high and still growing faster than anywhere else. A report by Ovum, a market research company, estimates that users will spend over $200 billion on m-commerce products and services by 2005, and that of the 500m mobile e-commerce customers in 2005, only 22% will be in North America.

MEATSPACE
The physical world, as described by participants in ONLINE conversations. Contrasts with CYBERSPACE.

MEGABYTE
A unit of data storage, equivalent to about 1m BYTES. Generally, a megabyte is considered to be equivalent to 2 to the 20th power bytes, or 1,048,576. Some authorities, however, claim that for purposes of data storage and transmission a megabyte is exactly 1m bytes. A HACKER would argue that only the first definition is correct, as bytes should logically be measured in powers of 2.

MELISSA
See VIRUS.

MEME
An idea, skill or habit passed from person to person. The term was coined in 1976 by Richard Dawkins, an English biologist, in his book *The Selfish Gene*. Dawkins speculated that memes are

to cultural information what genes are to genetic information and might thus play a crucial role in the evolution of the human brain and language. The Internet is seen by some as a new mechanism for the rapid dispersal of memes.

MICROPAYMENT

A small amount of money used to buy goods or services over the Internet. Micropayment systems are designed to allow CONTENT to be purchased in small quantities – one magazine article, say, or a single track from a CD – without the need to supply credit card details for every transaction. Instead, an electronic wallet on the buyer's PC transfers the requisite sum of money to the vendor in token form, and the vendor later reclaims the actual cash from a third-party bank.

This form of E-CASH is secure and convenient, but micropayments have not yet become popular with sellers of information. There is, as yet, no KILLER APP or trend-setting model, and many developers of micropayment technology are moving into other areas of E-COMMERCE. One problem with micropayments is keeping the cost of performing the transaction lower than the cost of the goods being exchanged. A bigger stumbling block is the subscription-based model that has become widely adopted among websites for text-based services, especially in the United States. The money obtained from credit card-based transactions and advertising sales is a more reliable source of revenue than an unpredictable stream of buyers paying a few cents each for content. In Europe, where credit cards are not as strongly entrenched, micropayments may have a rosier future.

MICROSOFT

A software company. Despite a general feeling that it is impossible for any one organisation to own the Internet, none is likely to come closer than Microsoft. Much has been made of Bill Gates's apparent failure to appreciate the importance of the Internet in 1995, when Microsoft seemed irreversibly committed to its proprietary

Microsoft Network (MSN). But its subsequent turnaround surprised even those observers accustomed to Gates's willingness and ability to change the direction of his business.

Within months of the launch of the first version of NETSCAPE'S NAVIGATOR, Microsoft had bought a BROWSER from a rival company, ditched its original plans for MSN and embarked on a massive phase of growth by acquisition and development that shows no sign of stopping. In less than five years, the firm that made a fortune from its MS-DOS and WINDOWS products has taken control of the browser market from Netscape, the company that invented it. It has acquired or invested in a bewildering array of Internet and communications companies, to the extent that it has at least a foot – and often several limbs – in every door. In the process, it has attracted the ire of the Department of Justice (DOJ) in the United States and more or less every company with which it does business – even those with which it does not directly compete, such as PC manufacturers.

Microsoft's dour and unflattering antitrust battle in the courts in 1999 highlighted the extent to which it has dominated its business partners and competitors with the ubiquitous Windows. But Judge Jackson's decision in April 2000 that the company had illegally distorted competition in Internet markets has not clarified its future. Many people, including US government lawyers, have called for the company to be broken up into competing divisions – "Baby Bills". At the very least, it will almost certainly be forbidden to distribute its browser with its OPERATING SYSTEM or other applications.

Microsoft's success with its browser has to some extent obscured the company's failures with its other Internet ventures. The most expensive of these to date is MSN, which has undergone many transitions in an attempt to make it successful and profitable. Its several manifestations have delivered a confusing mixture of Internet access, original CONTENT, licensed content and, most recently, PORTALS. At the same time, much to Microsoft's annoyance, rivals such as AOL have demonstrated that a carefully considered combination of these can be deadly in the right hands.

MIME

Multipurpose Internet Mail Extensions. MIME extends the text-only capabilities of the original Internet E-MAIL PROTOCOL SMTP, allowing people to exchange different kinds of information such as sound, video and still images. Many e-mail clients can encode and decode a file ATTACHMENT in the MIME format, and most BROWSERS can display MIME-encoded files; but users still fall foul of these encoding schemes. A file sent in MIME format can only be read by software that also speaks MIME, which is a problem for owners of programs that only understand other algorithms such as UUENCODE. Such incompatibilities are often the cause of those long, mystifying e-mails full of garbage.

MIRROR SITE

An exact copy of a website or FTP server. Many sites that offer files for downloading operate mirror sites at other locations, to reduce traffic on local servers and speed DOWNLOAD times for people a long way from the original source of the files. Many American websites, for example, offer mirror sites in several European countries. Small organisations, which may have limited Internet connectivity or slow hardware, often set up mirrors on larger or faster sites.

MISSION CREEP

Describes a phenomenon whereby projects expand ever further in scope as the deadline approaches. Widely encountered in companies developing websites, mission creep is often to blame for the bloated, inefficient and above all delayed nature of the resulting products.

MODEM

ACRONYM for modulator-demodulator, a device that translates a stream of digital data created by a computer into the curious squeaking and hissing sounds that can be transmitted across phone lines. Most subscribers to Internet services use modems to connect to their ISPs across the public telephone network, and nearly all PCs are now equipped with modems as standard. Ordinary modem-based connections have maximum speeds of 56KBPS, once considered almost embarrassingly fast but now hobbled by the increasing complexity of modern websites. Faster connections, such as ADSL and cable, use special "modems" – not, technically, quite the same thing – that can handle transmission at megabit speeds and higher.

MOORE'S LAW

A principle established in 1975 by Gordon Moore, co-founder of Intel, describing the rapid growth in the power of computer microprocessors over time. Officially, Moore's Law states that the circuit density or capacity of semiconductor chips doubles every 18 months, or quadruples every three years. (Moore's original 1965 article in an American magazine, *Electronics*, observed that the complexity of such chips roughly doubled every year, but he revised his predictions a decade later.) So far, it has proved to be not just an accurate measure of the development of computer chips but also a barometer for an entire industry.

Moore himself predicts that his law will run out of steam in 2012, when 1 billion transistors will be squeezed on to a processor and the limits of current chip fabrication technology are finally reached. Variants of it have been applied to everything from software to the web, both of which have grown even faster than the processors they rely on. The web grew from 10,000 sites at the beginning of 1995 to 4.5m sites by mid-1999.

MOSAIC

The first BROWSER that displayed more than plain text, developed at the NCSA by Marc Andreessen and others in 1993. Mosaic's appearance is widely credited with stimulating the tremendous interest in the WORLD WIDE WEB, until then a text-based academic curiosity. Andreessen and his team later used Mosaic as the template for the first NETSCAPE browser.

> *By the power vested in me by nobody in particular, alpha/beta version 0.5 of NCSA's Motif-based networked information systems and World Wide Web browser, X Mosaic, is hereby released.*
> Usenet post by Marc Andreessen, announcing the arrival of the first graphical browser

Mozilla

Originally the codename for NETSCAPE's first BROWSER, Mozilla was the name given to the company's dinosaur-like mascot. Most recently and importantly, it has been use to describe the family of web browsers based on the OPEN-SOURCE NAVIGATOR code. The Mozilla project is run as a independent group within Netscape, which moderates the development of improvements to the original browser code. Mozilla suffered some major setbacks in 1999 when many of the project's leading lights resigned, citing dissatisfaction with progress and company culture following the AOL takeover in 1998.

MP3

A format for recording near CD-quality music. Short for MPEG 1 Layer 3, an MP3 file is a music track that has been encoded and compressed for electronic distribution or storage. MP3's great trick is to squeeze musical recording into less than 10% of the space it would occupy if recorded in a standard format such as WINDOWS wav. Thus a four-minute song, which as a wav file might occupy 50 MEGABYTES of disk space, uses only 4 megabytes in its MP3 form. This highly efficient COMPRESSION has made MP3 the format of choice for so-called music pirates, who can record and distribute entire CDs across the Internet quickly and efficiently. Many NEWSGROUPS and websites are devoted to the dissemination of illegally recorded music, and the phenomenon has spawned a new generation of inexpensive hardware devices capable of storing and playing dozens of MP3 tracks. MP3 files are especially popular with students, most of whom have free high-speed access to the Internet and can thus download enormous amounts of music in a short time.

Estimates of the cost of MP3 piracy vary, but it is reckoned to be a small percentage of record companies' annual profits. In early 2000, however, the first evidence emerged that the phenomenon might be about to make a much bigger dent. A survey in the United States showed a drop of 4% in music sales within five miles of university campuses, in stores that historically account for 50% of all offline music sales. Rather than seeking ways to reduce these losses by embracing MP3 technology, the big labels have reacted to the threat by refusing to allow artists to distribute their music electronically and cracking down on allegedly illicit MP3 distribution services such as the ingenious NAPSTER. A consortium of companies from the music and computer industries formed the Secure Digital Music Initiative (SDMI) in late 1998, with the aim of creating software and hardware-based ENCRYPTION technologies that would make the illicit copying and distribution of music impossible. But their efforts to put this genie back in its bottle are being undermined by the sheer weight of support for MP3 and a new generation of music companies running MP3-based distribution services from their websites. CRACKERS, too, are sure to see any new music encryption system as an irresistible target.

You can make more money in this new era of "free" digital music. But only if you break free of label mind control.
Jaron Lanier

MPEG

Motion Picture Experts Group. MPEG systems encode and compress digital sound and video files to a format that can easily be stored on CDs or transmitted across networks. Several varieties of MPEG encoding exist, each tailored to a specific task. Some, such as MPEG 2, are especially useful for video applications, and MPEG 1 Layer 3 (MP3) is an elegant and efficient way of storing music.

MSN

Short for the Microsoft Network, an umbrella term for MICROSOFT's dial-up Internet access and ONLINE CONTENT business. Inspired by the success of AOL in the early 1990s – modest at that time – MSN started life as a proprietary NETWORK designed to attract people interested in electronic services and original content. Interest was initially so great that TCI, an American cable company, paid £125m for a 20% stake in the service before it had launched.

Originally accessible only to WINDOWS 95 users who dialled a local number for access to MSN's SERVERS, the service was slow to attract content providers, with the result that subscribers stayed away in their droves. Nonetheless, Microsoft persisted with its proprietary approach until well into 1996, when it became clear that the World Wide Web was where people wanted to be. Several changes of strategy quickly followed, in which Microsoft began to offer Internet access as part of a series of differently priced and confusingly wrapped packages. MSN's latest incarnation, based on a simple dial-up access model and a free-to-all customisable PORTAL, is its stablest to date; but it is not, and never will be, the all-conquering electronic medium for which Bill Gates and his generals had such high early hopes.

MUD

Short for multi-user dungeon (or, sometimes, dimension). A MUD is in essence a large, structured real-time CHAT room, in which participants, usually referred to as players, take part in role-playing games. Typically, a player will adopt a character taken from a sword-and-sorcery list of knights, dwarves, princesses and dragons. Once logged on to the system, players navigate through locations that might include rooms, forests or tunnels; negotiate a variety of traps and puzzles; grapple with the intricacies of the local bartering systems; and, generally, spend a long time doing nothing much.

MUDS were for many years the leading cause of computer addiction among students, for whom such fantasy worlds represented an attractive alternative to lectures. These days, simpler chat rooms and E-MAIL probably account for more wasted hours on campus, but research into MUDS and their OBJECT-ORIENTED cousins, called MOOS, continues as the interest in ONLINE VIRTUAL worlds grows. The flexibility offered by MOO languages has encouraged many people to immerse themselves more fully in these environments, perhaps by adopting a different gender, a different personality or even a different species. Such behaviour has inevitably attracted the attention of social scientists and behavioural psychologists, several of whom have written scholarly books attempting to explain it. More useful works have examined the possible extension of MUD and MOO technology into education, teleworking and even medicine.

MULTICASTING

The transmission of messages from a single sender to many recipients. Multicasting may be as simple as sending a daily newsletter from a website to several hundred subscribers, or as complex as updating the software on thousands of machines on a global corporate NETWORK. A specific kind of multicasting is used on the MBONE, a high-speed portion of the Internet designed for the delivery of large video and audio files such as live concerts.

MULTIMEDIA

The combination of different types of media, such as text, audio, video and animations, into some sort of informational whole that can be displayed on a computer. The role of multimedia in computing has undergone many transformations since its early days. Once a clumsy novelty used merely to entertain, it benefited greatly from more powerful hardware and more imaginative software design tools. Its use in CD-ROM-based educational software, particularly encyclopedias, helped to illustrate its potential. The much-vaunted CD-ROM market proved to be an expensive illusion for many firms involved in producing educational CDs in the late 1990s, but the promise of multimedia is stronger than ever because of the Internet and its ability to deliver original CONTENT to a widely distributed audience. The commercially successful implementation of multimedia technology, however, depends entirely on significantly greater BANDWIDTH than is currently widely available – and, some would argue, rather more taste on the part of its designers.

MULTIPLEXING
The combining of several signals in the same communications channel, usually with the aim of increasing the amount of data that can be transmitted. Several types of multiplexing exist, each designed for a particular signal and cable type. Analog signals, for example, are combined using frequency-division multiplexing (FDM), in which the BANDWIDTH is divided into parallel channels of different frequencies. Digital signals can be transmitted using time-division multiplexing (TDM), in which the signals are carried using alternating time slots. On FIBRE OPTIC networks, multiple signals are transmitted as light split into different wavelengths, a process known as wavelength-division multiplexing (WDM). This technique is being widely investigated to improve the speed of Internet BACKBONES.

MULTI-USER
Describes an aspect of a computer system that can be accessed by more than one individual at a time. Many OPERATING SYSTEMS (and all NETWORK operating systems), such as UNIX and WINDOWS NT, are designed to allow many people to log in at the same time and access the same network resources – a particularly important consideration for web SERVERS. Similarly, some application programs, especially DATABASES, let people work together on the same data sets, using record-locking techniques to prevent entries being overwritten.

NAME SERVER

A computer on the Internet that tracks the relationship between IP ADDRESSES and DOMAIN NAMES. Name servers are responsible for translating alphanumeric E-MAIL and web addresses into the 32-BIT numbers computers use to find each other on the Internet, thus making sure that messages arrive at the right place.

NAPSTER

An Internet-based system for distributing music in the digital MP3 format. Napster allows owners of digitally encoded music to share their collections with other users of the NETWORK, simply by publishing a list of the files on their computer and allowing anyone else using the software to download the music to their own PC. The simplicity of the software and the openness of the network has attracted millions of users, not all of whom have a deeply entrenched respect for COPYRIGHT law; this has led to widespread condemnation of the system by music industry bodies and recording artists. In April 2000 the rock band Metallica collected the names of 300,000 users it claimed were illegally distributing its copyright music and forced Napster to remove them from the system. Many users promptly re-registered under different names. The company remains sanguine in the face of some heavyweight opposition, advising its users on counter-notification procedures to get themselves reinstated and continuing to release new versions of the software.

NASDAQ

Short for National Association of Securities Dealers Automated Quotation system. Most of the high-tech companies in the United States trade on NASDAQ, which has consequently become one of the most powerful engines driving the Silicon Valley economy.

NAVIGATION

The process of finding your way around a website. The provision of adequate navigation tools is one of the biggest challenges facing website developers, who must consider not just how to guide visitors from the HOME PAGE of their site but also how to indicate their exact location within it. Well-designed sites provide a visual equivalent of the "You are here" arrows seen on maps – often a necessity if the visitor has arrived at a deeply buried page from a SEARCH ENGINE or directory.

Navigation is inevitably an inexact science on the web, and although organisations such as the W3C provide some firm guidelines, there are no generally agreed rules. This explains the great diversity of mechanisms used, from the simplest HTML pages via frames-based designs to complex JAVA or JAVASCRIPT-driven interfaces. But navigation is generally improving across websites as a whole, as a result of better development tools and the willingness of the web COMMUNITY to borrow good ideas and good code.

NAVIGATOR

A BROWSER produced by NETSCAPE. Once the undisputed market leader, Navigator's innovation and technical excellence made it the browser of choice for millions of neophyte Internet users. These characteristics have not been enough to maintain its dominance, and its market share has been gradually whittled away by INTERNET EXPLORER since MICROSOFT began giving it away with the WINDOWS OPERATING SYSTEM. Some estimates now rate Navigator's market share at 20% or less.

The software's future is now in the hands of AOL, which may lack the distribution mechanism of its giant competitor but could prove a match for it in terms of marketing know-how. A much-delayed version of Navigator, designed to be easily adapted for use with devices such as set-top boxes and even mobile phones, was released in mid-2000. (See MOZILLA.)

NC

See NETWORK COMPUTER.

NCSA

The National Centre For Supercomputing Applications. Based at the University of Illinois, the NCSA is a research organisation specialising in high-performance computer applications in many fields. It is best known for its work in developing MOSAIC, the first graphical web BROWSER.

NERD

A generally pejorative term for someone of above-average intelligence but who has poorly developed social skills and is sartorially challenged. Nerds are often portrayed as being shy, badly dressed and incapable of forming normal relationships, especially with members of the opposite sex. Real or not, this image has shifted somewhat as the realisation has grown that nerds are among the most powerful people in our society. An oft-cited example of this is Bill Gates, for whom nerdism has not proved a significant disability. Several explanations for the word's origin have been proposed, the most interesting being that it is the name of a character in Dr Seuss's 1950 book *If I Ran The Zoo.*

And then, just to show them, I'll sail to Ka-Troo
And bring back an It-Kutch, a Preep and a Proo
A Nerkle, a Nerd, and a Seersucker, too!
From *If I Ran The Zoo*, by Dr Seuss (1950)

NETHEAD

An engineer or other individual with a strong belief in the power of intelligent, IP-based digital networks over the final networks run by telephone companies. Contrast with BELLHEAD.

NETIQUETTE

The conventions of politeness on USENET. Many relate to the niceties of posting messages in NEWS-GROUPS; for example, advertising beef products in alt.food.vegan is a clear breach of netiquette. Individual newsgroups often have their own conventions, which are usually explained in the group's FAQ. The penalties for not observing netiquette are generally minor, although repeat offenders may find that life ONLINE suddenly becomes extremely uncomfortable. Lucky ones may get away with a FLAME; less fortunate individuals have found their credit card details posted to Usenet, or worse.

NETSCAPE

A company that played a major role in creating worldwide enthusiasm for the Internet. It started life in 1994 with a single product and a handful of programmers. By the time the company went public just 16 months later it was worth $2 billion. That single product, the NAVIGATOR BROWSER, deserves much of the credit for generating the early interest in the WORLD WIDE WEB. Founded by Marc Andreessen, a whizz-kid programmer responsible for MOSAIC, and Jim Clark, the brains behind Silicon Graphics, Netscape quickly became an important symbol and inspiration for the burgeoning Internet industry.

First indications that it might struggle to keep its head above water came with MICROSOFT'S aggressive entry into the browser market in 1995. Netscape, which had a single source of revenue, was forced to charge for corporate versions of Navigator. But Microsoft could afford to give its software away, first on its website and then, much more damagingly, as part of the WINDOWS OPERATING SYSTEM. What started as a 90% market share has been slowly but steadily whittled away, and recent surveys suggest that it might have slipped to 20%.

NETWARE

A NETWORK OPERATING SYSTEM developed by NOVELL. For many years Netware was the undisputed champion of PC-based corporate networks, owning 75% of the market for multi-user operating systems. Weakened by an ill-advised venture into the office software market and two management changes, the company struggled to maintain leadership over MICROSOFT'S WINDOWS NT product, and its market share declined disastrously in the mid-1990s. In recent versions of Netware great improvements have been made in its use of Internet technology, especially as regards INTRANETS, although surveys indicate that it lost its number two position in corporate SERVER markets to LINUX in early 2000.

NETWORK

A collection of people or things, linked together to share information or resources. The Internet can be viewed as one vast network of computers, although it is probably more useful to see it as merely a huge number of smaller networks connected in an arbitrary and self-organising manner.

All the most promising technologies making their debut now are chiefly due to communication between computers – that is, to connections rather than to computations. And since communication is the basis of culture, fiddling at this level is indeed momentous.
Kevin Kelly

NETWORK COMPUTER

A low-cost INFORMATION APPLIANCE based on a minimalist design and a centralised networking philosophy. The brainchild of Oracle's Larry Ellison, the network computer (NC) – an example of a THIN CLIENT – promised to change the MICROSOFT-driven computing model radically by removing the bells and whistles, such as hard disks and CD-ROM drives, from a desktop computer and managing its resources centrally. NCS can run small, fast, BROWSER-driven applications based on JAVA or another suitable system and thus do not need big, complex OPERATING SYSTEMS like WINDOWS. Every time users need a new version of a software program they DOWNLOAD a copy from a SERVER rather than install it locally from disk or CD-ROM, massively reducing distribution costs. Such machines need not be tied to the Intel processor, with the increased freedom and reduced costs that this implies. Best of all, network computers should theoretically be a fraction of the cost of a fully-specified PC.

The concept sounds attractive, but sales have been in hundreds of thousands rather than the millions Wintel-busters (those who would like to see Microsoft's and Intel's hold on the industry reduced) would have liked. NCS have proved costlier than anticipated, selling at not much less than an all-singing, all-dancing, NETWORK-enabled PC. The cost of upgrading corporate networks with more advanced data storage and management software has also proved to be substantially more than expected; and not all NC/server combinations were quite as compatible as the original specification promised. The biggest hurdle for NCS has been the enduring appeal and usefulness of PCS, which despite their undoubted problems are not nearly as unpopular with the general public as they are with SUN MICROSYSTEMS and Oracle.

Despite these drawbacks, the NC model seems sure to become part of the landscape as information appliances of all kinds expand their capabilities and more devices become network-aware. A critical part of this process will be the long-promised hike in BANDWIDTH, especially in the home.

NETWORK EXTERNALITIES
An economic term describing the effect that new members of a NETWORK have on the existing ones. A network containing one fax machine is useless, but as the number of machines added to it increases, the more valuable each becomes. Thus the decision by a newcomer to subscribe to the fax network increases the value of all the other machines. This effect has been the driving force behind the Internet, which has become more and more useful as the number of people connecting to it has grown. It has also introduced another, equally interesting, phenomenon: the increasing value of knowledge. In the same way that the usefulness of a language depends on the number of people who speak it, so the usefulness of some kinds of information increases with their dissemi-

nation. This is one reason for the rapid rate of development of Internet technologies. (See also INCREASING RETURNS.)

NETWORK SOLUTIONS

A US-based organisation which registers new top-level domains. It was appointed to its role by the National Science Foundation in 1993, and held an exclusive licence to register the most popular type of Internet DOMAIN, .COM, until 1998, earning itself millions of dollars. Complaints about the company's monopoly led to investigation by the US Department of Commerce, and it has subsequently opened the registration process to limited competition on a trial basis.

NEW MEDIA

Forms of mass communications driven by the Internet and related technologies. New media differ from so-called old media, such as newspapers and television, primarily in that they are targetable and interactive. People and businesses are no longer restricted to mere consumer status but can be producers too, as the rapidly expanding web testifies.

NEWBIE

A newcomer to the Internet, or, more specifically, to USENET and its NEWSGROUPS. Newbies are widely reviled for their lack of NETIQUETTE and are discouraged from participating in some newsgroups. The term is sometimes used a put-down for otherwise experienced Usenetters who upset the locals.

NEWSGROUP

A discussion group on the USENET. Unlike CHAT rooms, newsgroups are not live; instead, questions and comments are posted to one of many Usenet servers and later redistributed around the rest of the NETWORK. Most ISPs provide a newsgroup feed, which pipes the contents of most of the 30,000 or so newsgroups to anyone who wants to take part in the discussions on offer. There are tens of thousands of newsgroups, each devoted to a specific and often highly unconventional set of interests, and anyone who has wondered about the ins and outs of beekeeping or the relationship between bondage and particle physics will find groups that answer their questions. This openness, and the fact that most newsgroups are unmoderated and unregulated, almost demands a robust attitude on behalf of the inhabitants, and the unwary can get some nasty surprises if they fail to observe NETI-QUETTE. Newsgroups have also attracted much attention as a primary source of PORNOGRAPHY, and much debate exists over whether or not ISPS should carry such groups. (See CENSORSHIP.)

NNTP

Network News Transport Protocol, the PROTOCOL used to manage traffic on USENET NEWSGROUPS. Most ISPS run an NNTP SERVER, which communicates with others like it to filter and filter the global collection of newsgroups. NNTP is the replacement for the UNIX UUCP (Unix-to-Unix Copy Protocol) found on older networks.

NODE

A HOST computer on a NETWORK. A node may be as simple as a standalone PC connected to the Internet across a dial-up connection or as complex as a SERVER delivering information to hundreds of machines.

NOTES

The software that popularised GROUPWARE. Lotus Notes was written by Ray Ozzie, who Bill Gates is said to have described as one of the five best programmers in the universe. It is based on central discussion DATABASES, which can include not just text-based E-MAIL messages but also spreadsheets, word-processed documents and many other kinds of business data. Notes lets people work together on these in real time, keeping track of who makes which changes and keeping everybody's copies updated automatically. Among its most important features is its ability to replicate its discussion databases remotely, thus ensuring that travelling workers always have access to the latest information.

Notes is used by thousands of companies worldwide to share knowledge and skills in many different business areas. Its critics cite its comparatively high cost and its proprietary nature as significant barriers, especially with the advent of INTRANETS. But Lotus has opened up the product significantly in the last few years, adopting several Internet standards and providing tools to access data held in Notes databases in different ways.

NOVELL

A software company, best known for its NETWARE NETWORK OPERATING SYSTEM. Novell's fortunes flagged seriously in the mid-1990s as large companies abandoned or overlooked Netware in favour of WINDOWS NT. The recruitment in 1997 of Eric Schmidt from SUN MICROSYSTEMS as chief executive and a timely, technically innovative upgrade to the core Netware product helped start a revival process.

NT

See WINDOWS NT.

OBJECT-ORIENTED

Describes a popular approach to programming, in which computer programs are built from software objects that do particular jobs. Objects often have functions that resemble those in the real world. A shopping-basket object on a website, for example, could keep track of how many items it carries and maintain a running total of their value. This approach has many benefits to programmers, in particular the ability to reuse sections of code to perform multiple tasks and allow different programs to co-operate with each other efficiently. The most popular languages for writing object-oriented software are C++ and JAVA. The latter was designed specifically for networked environments, and it is growing in importance as more INFORMATION APPLIANCES become NETWORK-friendly.

OFFLINE

See ONLINE.

1.0

Pronounced "one point oh", a term denoting the first version or iteration of something, usually a piece of software but often extended to websites, new hardware devices and even companies or strategies.

ONLINE

Connected to the Internet or another electronic service such as a BULLETIN BOARD. Its opposite, offline, denotes the lack of such a connection.

ONLINE AUCTION

The latest and, to date, most profitable form of consumer-driven E-COMMERCE. There are two broad categories of ONLINE auctions.

- The merchant auction involves a manufacturer or retailer offering goods for sale, often using an intermediate auction specialist, such as Quixell and Online Auctions in the UK. These auctions are popular because they provide an easy way

for buyer and seller to agree a price, especially for old stock or goods approaching the end of their shelf life, and because almost anything can be sold in this way: holidays, computers, cars or cameras.
- The personal auction provides a way for individuals to trade items with each other.

Online auctions have proved a big success with Internet users, largely because they do not rely on the fixed pricing favoured by most online retailers. Most sites run in much the same way as their real-world counterparts. Sellers post a description of their item for sale, set a closing date and an optional reserve price, and wait for customers to bid. Personal auctioneers make money by charging sellers an initial insertion fee and then taking a commission on the sale.

The biggest name in the personal auction field is eBay, founded in 1995 by Pierre Omidyar, following an observation by his wife, a collector of confectionery dispensers, that people with interests in specialist items should be able to trade them online. This has turned out to be one of the Internet's most persuasive ideas, as reflected in the large number of companies that have followed in eBay's path. But none has yet matched the enthusiasm of eBay's visitors, who line up online daily to trade millions of items for millions of dollars. Omidyar's COMMUNITY-building prowess has resulted in that most elusive of qualities in an Internet company – profitability. This has been achieved as a result of a business model requiring no storing of goods, no carriage costs and, indeed, no interaction at all with the items for sale. The company simply charges the "seller" a flat fee and a percentage of the sale price.

A certain risk is inevitably associated with online auctions, especially when dealing with individuals rather than companies. But the public has participated eagerly, helping eBay's stockmarket value to reach the dizzy heights of over $18 billion by mid-1999. Unsurprisingly, other organisations have not been slow to see the potential of auctions. YAHOO and AMAZON both offer auction services on their websites, and other SEARCH ENGINES and retailers were promising similar features in 2000.

The seven products bought most often on the web: books, software, music, travel, hardware, clothing and electronics.

ONLINE GAMING

The playing of computer games across a NETWORK connection, usually in competition with other players. Many games, especially those of the shoot-'em-up genre such as DOOM, are now designed to be played by lots of people simultaneously, either on the Internet or across a LOCAL AREA NETWORK. Players connect to a central computer, which controls the gaming environment and manages the interaction between the participants. Some kinds of online games, such as MUDS, are simple text-based programs demanding little by way of raw processing power but rather more by way of logic. More contemporary games typically involve complex 3D graphics, dramatic sound effects and a lot of physical interaction between players and their environment.

Online games can support hundreds or in some cases thousands of simultaneous players. Because of their complexity and high degree of realism, they have provided inspiration for researchers into new forms of VIRTUAL reality and even teleworking. Instead of dingy mazes full of axes and chainsaws, people are now building online offices full of filing cabinets and fax machines. Such is progress.

ONLINE SERVICE

A company offering electronic access to a variety of services besides those available from Internet service providers (ISPS). These often include exclusive CONTENT and special offers, proprietary CHAT rooms and other COMMUNITY facilities. Because these services typically use their own closed networks and communications services rather than public websites, their facilities are available only to subscribers.

The largest of the online services, sometimes called online service providers (OSPS), is AOL, which provides a wide array of goodies for subscribers alongside standard dial-up Internet access. The distinction between OSPS and ISPS has blurred in recent years, as many websites and PORTALS have begun to duplicate their offerings in a public environment. But the OSP model is clearly still working; AOL remains comfortably the largest service provider of any description.

OPEN PROFILING STANDARD

A system that gives website visitors more control over the information they provide about themselves. The Open Profiling Standard (OPS) allows the storage of personal information about someone in a secure electronic profile on their computer. These profiles can contain almost any sort of information – name, address, age, favourite football team, food allergies – which can then optionally be shared with websites that request it. (One important exception to this list is financial information, such as credit card details, which is more suitable for electronic wallets.)

A big advantage of the OPS over current systems is that it saves users from having to fill in the same web registration forms over and over again, an increasingly common and tiresome chore as sites request more information for their demographic DATABASES. The OPS also allows users to specify exactly what information they wish to divulge, to whom and for what purpose; whether it can be used in public surveys or sold on to third parties, for example.

OPEN SOURCE

A concept describing the development and distribution of software. The open source movement revolves around the idea that software evolves faster and becomes more stable as more people work on it. This idea has long been in practice in

O

the UNIX world, where code-sharing and co-development projects are common, but it is anathema to software companies, which like to develop their products in relative secrecy. One driving force behind the open source concept is the Open Source Initiative (OSI), a non-profit organisation. Software developers that wish to use the Open Source trademark must distribute their software and its SOURCE CODE for free. Much of the movement's inspiration comes from Richard Stallman, the man behind the FREE SOFTWARE FOUNDATION and creator of the legendary EMACS text editor, and Eric Raymond, whose paper "The Cathedral and the Bazaar" first brought the open source idea to the attention of commercial software vendors.

For proof that open-source development works look no further than LINUX, an OPERATING SYSTEM written by Linus Torvalds and subsequently tested and tweaked by tens of thousands of users united by the enabling technology of the Internet. The intense scrutiny to which Linux has been subjected by its hundreds of thousands of users has created a stable, bug-free system that now represents a substantial threat to MICROSOFT's flagship WINDOWS NT product. This is an extraordinary achievement for a piece of software that is free to anyone who wants it. The first commercial software house to follow the lead of Torvalds, Stallman and other luminaries was NETSCAPE, which in 1998 released the source code to its NAVIGATOR BROWSER into the public domain as the first stage of the MOZILLA project.

Provided the development co-ordinator has a medium at least as good as the Internet, and knows how to lead without coercion, many heads are inevitably better than one.
Eric Raymond

OPERA
A BROWSER made by a Norwegian software house and much admired for its small size and impressive speed, rare commodities in the modern software world.

OPERATING SYSTEM

The operating system is the most important part of any computer or NETWORK. Its main role is as an interpreter between the hardware itself – the processor, hard disks, video system, network cards, and so on – and the applications that are running on the computer which need access to those resources, such as E-MAIL programs, spreadsheets and DATABASES. Thus the operating system (often abbreviated to OS) must be able to speak the complex language of the chips that make up the computer, while also presenting a friendly face that human operators can understand.

This simple explanation belies the complexities of modern operating systems such as WINDOWS NT, MacOS and LINUX, which now have an extraordinary level of technical sophistication. As well as its responsibilities for managing the hardware and its peripherals (printers, CD-ROM drives, and so on), the OS must look after files, prevent programs from crashing each other, control network traffic and enforce security. This last item is a particularly important consideration in networked environments, where computers are susceptible to attack by CRACKERS, VIRUSES and other malicious entities. Unsurprisingly, operating systems are prime targets for certain crackers, who delight in exposing flaws in the code, especially of Microsoft's Windows NT. Operating systems, specifically those produced by Microsoft, have also acquired a significant political importance (see MICROSOFT).

OSP

Online Service Provider (see ONLINE SERVICE).

PACKET

A unit of data used to send information across the Internet. Most types of NETWORK communications use the Transport Control Protocol (TCP) layer of the TCP/IP PROTOCOL to split messages into a number of discrete packets before transmitting them. Each packet contains the address of its destination and a number denoting its place in the sequence. Some kinds of packets also include information about what sort of data they are carrying, which allows the network to prioritise different sorts of data; for example, sending time-critical video data ahead of text.

Packets have some significant advantages compared with continuous streams of BITS. Packets from the same original message can travel by different routes across the network, each taking the path that is least crowded at the time of transmission. Once they have all arrived at their destination they are reassembled into the correct order. Networks that use packets can also transmit parts of several different messages at the same time. The disadvantage of packet-based networks is that the process of splitting up and reassembling messages imposes a time delay and a processing overhead. The degree to which this matters varies according to the type of packet. ATM networks, which use a small packet size, have more work to do and thus impose a greater overhead.

PACKET-SWITCHED

Describes a NETWORK that sends data one PACKET at a time, rather than as a continuous stream. Unlike CIRCUIT-SWITCHED networks, which depend on exclusive use of a connection, packet-switched networks can share out the available BANDWIDTH to several communications simultaneously.

PANS

A multipurpose ACRONYM, originally designed to operate in parallel with POTS but now assuming a life of its own. Purists argue that PANS stands for Public Access Network Services, part of a vision of a society in which everyone has access to information sources, regardless of social circumstances, as a basic democratic right. Less worthy sources claim it as the short form of Pretty Amazing Network Services, a general description of new high-speed communications networks such as ADSL. Everybody else thinks that it stands for Pretty Awesome New Stuff, an umbrella term covering more or less every post-POTS technological development.

PASSWORD

A sequence of characters required to LOG IN or otherwise gain access to a computer system. Despite widespread publicity about the importance of choosing a secure password, many systems and networks are cracked by deducing the passwords to people's computers. Current theory suggests that passwords should consist of both letters and numbers, as these are much harder to guess than even random combinations of one or the other. Birthdays, telephone numbers, or names of spouses or pets are obvious targets, as are obscene words, cartoon characters, religious expressions and actors' names. Some security experts even advise against choosing any word that is in any dictionary, as programs exist that can try every word from all the most popular lexicons.

PDA

Personal Digital Assistant, an electronic device that helps people manage information. PDAs take many forms, although all include an LCD screen for displaying telephone numbers, diary dates and E-MAIL. Some, such as Psion's popular machines, have their own built-in keyboard. Others, including 3Com's Palm range, rely on a simple form of handwriting recognition for data input. Most recently, MICROSOFT's WINDOWS CE (a cutdown version of its desktop OPERATING SYSTEM) has found its way on to machines made by several vendors. Increasingly, PDAs are being used as fully fledged INFORMATION APPLIANCES, and are equipped with e-mail clients and web BROWSERS as standard.

PDF

Portable Document Format, a file created by Adobe's ACROBAT software. PDF files are designed for distributing documents electronically, and thus contain original fonts, graphics and other design elements that faithfully record the layout of the original. They can even contain audio and video sequences. PDF is especially suitable for distributing documents by E-MAIL, as it requires the creation of one extremely cheap electronic file rather than the expensive printing of hundreds of paper versions.

PERL

A flexible programming language widely used in Internet environments, especially websites. Written by Larry Wall, Perl is popular with programmers because it is fast, comparatively easy to learn and, as a bonus, free. Perl programmes will run on any PLATFORM without modifications, so the same code can be used on a WINDOWS NT box, a UNIX server or a Macintosh. Many CGI SCRIPTS are written in Perl.

PGP

Pretty Good Privacy, an encryption program that the US government tried to ban. Developed by Phil Zimmerman in the early 1990s, PGP has become a byword for E-MAIL security. It has also been the source of some controversy, following its international distribution in defiance of an American ban on the export of strong encryption software and its unauthorised use of the RSA algorithm. Zimmerman sold PGP to Network Associates, a software company, in 1997. Its new owners exported the source code to the Netherlands in book form, rather than as actual code, to circumvent US laws governing the export of so-called munitions, and an international version is currently on sale. PGP is thus one of few programs whose international versions are as secure as their American equivalents. (See ENCRYPTION.)

PICS

Platform for Internet Content Selection, a way of rating the content of websites. PICS was designed to give parents, schools and companies control over things that their charges view on the Internet. Although conceived primarily to prevent access to PORNOGRAPHY and hate speech, PICS can be used to rate lots of other things, such as books or films. Although the primary responsibility for rating sites rests with their owners, third parties can rate them too, so an anti-racism organisation could maintain and rate a list of sites containing racist material. The PICS software on a home computer could then be configured to check that list before allowing access to any of the sites.

Many software companies have built support for PICS into their BROWSERS and BLOCKING SOFTWARE products, enabling parents or NETWORK administrators to rate CONTENT on several different levels and allow access accordingly. The problem facing PICS and RSAC is that despite their elegant design and relative ease of implementation, almost nobody uses them. Site owners have not shown the hoped-for public-spiritedness, and the web is just too big for third parties to rate it reliably. PICS will probably not go away, but its proponents may have to look for more dependable means of governing access to undesirable material.

PING

A small program used to check for the presence and response time of a remote computer. Most OPERATING SYSTEMS are supplied with a ping program for testing Internet connections. The term is also used in reference to people, as in "I haven't heard from Angus for a while. I'll ping him this evening".

PING STORM

A flood of large PACKETS sent to a computer by a PING program, either to test the machine's ability to manage large volumes of traffic or, occasionally, deliberately to cause it to malfunction. The malicious use of ping in this way, sometimes referred to as the Ping of Death, has shut down several large networks.

PKI
See PUBLIC KEY INFRASTRUCTURE.

PLATFORM
Broadly, the combination of an OPERATING SYSTEM and a processor to form a system on which application programs can run. Nowadays, the term is often used to refer just to the operating system, an assumption having been made that the processor in question is made by Intel. Historically, different versions of the same computer program have often been written to run on different platforms, creating big headaches for software developers in the process. NETSCAPE NAVIGATOR, for example, runs on around 20 different platforms. The JAVA language promised to bring platform independence to the software world but has met with limited success to date.

PLUG-IN
A small piece of software that extends the capabilities of another, larger program. The most common use of plug-ins is made by BROWSERS, which use them to display particular types of data, such as animations and video. Many vendors of MULTIMEDIA development tools distribute plug-ins for users to play their creations. (See also HELPER APPLICATION.)

PNG
Portable Network Graphics, a kind of graphics file designed for creating pictures for web pages. Despite a good COMPRESSION scheme and considerable technical superiority, PNG has so far failed to capture the imagination of web designers, who generally rely on GIF and JPEG files for illustrating their works. One of PNG's weaknesses is that it does not directly support animations, one of GIF's strongest features, making it unsuitable for eye-catching contemporary BANNER ADVERTISING.

POP

Point of Presence, an access point on the Internet. Each ISP has at least one POP, to which users dial in when they want to establish an Internet connection. Some big ISPs, such as COMPUSERVE, have hundreds of POPs in dozens of countries, ensuring that subscribers can always make a local call to check their E-MAIL. Not to be confused with POP3.

POP3

The latest version of the Post Office Protocol, a standard for retrieving E-MAIL. POP3 is a CLIENT/SERVER PROTOCOL in which the client, an e-mail program, periodically checks a SERVER for new mail. Most mail programs now support POP3, and several web-based e-mail services such as Hotmail can collect messages from POP3 mailboxes. (See also IMAP.)

In September 1999, 12.5m Americans visited pornographic websites from their homes. Only 74% of them were male.

PORNOGRAPHY

One of the Internet's biggest businesses. As the world's media never tire of pointing out, pornography is widely available on the net, in both commercialised subscription form and for free. Regulating it has turned out to be a much trickier business than finding it, as every government that has tried to do so has found. Blanket CENSORSHIP, in particular, has proved to be impossible. This is excellent news for the pornography industry, which has taken to the web with relish. Forrester, an American research company, estimated the market for "adult content" to be nearly $1 billion in 1998, about 10% of the total amount spent on E-COMMERCE.

The traffic generated by porn sellers would make any ONLINE business green with envy. The most popular paid-for sites in the United States attract millions of users every month, and so-called free sites measure visitors in tens of millions. A great strength of successful pay sites is their ability to convert VIEWERS into paying customers, thanks to a strategy involving lots of free samples and some superior video and WEBCAM technology. Those who have set up pornography sites on the web have shown little interest in ratings standards such as PICS and RSAC, and manufacturers of BLOCKING SOFTWARE have little hope, in practice, of keeping track of new porn websites.

PORTABILITY

A characteristic of a program which can run on any PLATFORM without modification. It may sound simple to achieve but it is extremely hard to engineer because of enormous differences between OPERATING SYSTEMS and processors and a general unwillingness by their developers to co-operate. JAVA, SUN MICROSYSTEMS's programming language, promised to deliver this Holy Grail of computing and, maybe, break MICROSOFT's stranglehold on the personal computer industry in the process. But despite much public wishful thinking on Sun's behalf, only the simplest Java programs have turned out to be truly portable.

PORTAL

An electronic gateway to the WORLD WIDE WEB. The portal is really an extension of the SEARCH ENGINE idea, but instead of providing lists of sites matching someone's search criteria it relies on a selection process to choose starter sites that new users might be interested in visiting. The biggest portals are run by some of the net's most visible brands, including AOL, YAHOO, MSN, Excite and LYCOS. A measure of the importance of portals is that these five companies' sites were the most visited anywhere on the web in April 2000, according to statistics from Nielsen Netratings.

Portals are the latest leg of the endless quest for ways of attracting web surfers and (much harder) making them come back again. Their owners claim to achieve this STICKINESS by providing a range of information services and entertainment so essential that visitors are irresistibly drawn to return. These might include a directory of other sites, a search facility, a weather service, CHAT rooms, free E-MAIL and a selection of sports, cinema and other entertainment sites. To maximise their exposure, ISPS and BROWSER manufacturers invariably preconfigure their browsers to load their portal sites automatically when they run, thus more or less guaranteeing that a known number of people will visit the site at least once, which is important in attracting advertisers.

The problem with portals is that they necessarily provide a lowest-common-denominator guide to the web, and visitors quickly tire of their contents once they figure out how to find their way around the new medium. Quick-thinking entrepreneurs have already moved on to the next big thing in portal concepts, the VORTAL. Other forms of portal are steadily emerging, including the mortal, a site dedicated to mobile computing resources, and even the snortal, a site updating the scratch-and-sniff card concept for the digital age.

PORT SCAN

A digital probe sent by a CRACKER attempting to break into someone else's computer. Port scans look for open conduits into a computer via its Internet connection, attempting to discover whether or not an exploitable weakness exists or whether a TROJAN HORSE program is installed. Port-scanning software is widely available on the Internet, most of it used by SCRIPT KIDDIES to disrupt hapless users' activities. Some Trojans such as SubSeven have their own port scanning programs, and other more powerful tools such as nmap provide stealthier and more insidious facilities for identifying computers that are vulnerable to attack. The best form of defence against port scanners is a FIREWALL. Many new software-only firewalls are now available to protect individual users as well as company NETWORKS.

POTS

Plain Old Telephone Service – in short, what you get when you pick up a telephone (see PANS).

The telephone has too many shortcomings to be seriously considered as a means of communication.

Western Union internal memo, 1876

PPP

Point-to-Point Protocol, a way for two computers connected by a serial interface to communicate with each other. The most common use of PPP is to connect a computer to an ISP across a MODEM and telephone line. Compare with SLIP, an older and more error-prone way of managing serial connections.

PPTP

Point-to-Point Tunnelling Protocol (see TUNNELLING).

PRIVATE KEY

A type of KEY used to decode encrypted messages, known only to the sender and recipient of a message. Some ENCRYPTION algorithms such as DES rely on a single private key, using the same string of characters to both encode and decode a message. This technique has some disadvantages, the main one being the difficulty of exchanging the key between the sender and recipient and figuring out how it should itself be encrypted. If the key is inadvertently intercepted or revealed by either party, the message can instantly be decrypted. Another problem is that every message must have its own unique key, selected from (in the case of DES) one of tens of quadrillions of alternatives. Contrast this with PUBLIC KEY CRYPTOGRAPHY, in which only two keys are ever needed (one public, one private) no matter how many messages are generated.

PROTOCOL

A set of rules that determines how two computers should communicate with each other. Many dif-

---

ferent protocols are used on the Internet because the rules for each form of communication it allows vary considerably. E-MAIL, for example, requires a particular set of commands to be understood by both sender and receiver; these commands are described by the POP3 and SMTP protocols, among others. Similarly, the TCP protocol describes how senders and receivers should manage the transmission of PACKETS across a NETWORK. Other common Internet protocols are HTTP, IP and FTP.

PROXY SERVER

A computer that controls traffic between a LOCAL AREA NETWORK and the wider Internet. Many companies use proxy servers to regulate access to Internet services such as the web, FTP and TELNET. When a computer on the LAN makes a request for an Internet service the request passes through the proxy server, which then decides how to deal with it. If the request is for a prohibited service, the proxy server returns an error. If the service is allowed, it is either passed on to the Internet server as usual or in the case of web requests to a local CACHE, from where previously downloaded pages can be more quickly accessed. Proxy servers give companies a fine degree of control over their Internet access policies. They can track every request from the NETWORK, for example, including IP addresses and even keystrokes. They are often used to prevent files from travelling in or out of a corporate network. (See also FIREWALL.)

PUBLIC KEY CRYPTOGRAPHY

A cryptographic system in which messages are encrypted with a KEY split into two parts. One of these parts is publicly available and the other is private. A message sent with one kind of key can only be encrypted by the other. Public key cryptography uses complex mathematical algorithms based on large prime numbers, and in its most advanced forms is regarded as more or less unbreakable even with the most powerful computers. (See ENCRYPTION.)

PUBLIC KEY INFRASTRUCTURE

A complex way of administering large public key ENCRYPTION schemes. The use of encryption to conceal or authenticate the contents of messages between two people is simple enough, but it becomes significantly harder as the number of regular communicants grows. A global company doing business electronically, such as a bank, must find a way not just to publish the public keys of everybody on the network (including employees, suppliers and customers), but also to evaluate the extent to which everyone should trust each other. Anne may trust Bill, for example, who in turn trusts Carla; but Carla may not trust either Anne or Bill, and so requires each of them to prove that their credentials are still valid every time they communicate.

As the number of people in this web grows, the problem of managing the relationships becomes severe. Public key infrastructure (PKI) schemes handle this with hierarchical certification programs, which associate public keys with individuals or organisations, and validation schemes, which verify that a certificate is still valid. There are many other problems for PKI designers to solve; one is irrefutability, or the ability to say with certainty that an individual definitely signed a document or wrote a message (see DIGITAL SIGNATURE). Such issues have many legal and social aspects as well as technical ones, further increasing the difficulty of implementing PKI on a wide scale.

PUSH MEDIA

CONTENT that is delivered automatically, rather than waiting for someone to come and get it. Push solves a problem common to many people who use the Internet, who know exactly what information they want but still have to go out and get it every time they need it. By subscribing to a push-based service, the information can be delivered straight to their computer as it becomes available. Push is an especially attractive technology for advertisers, who can be sure that viewers of their material have actually requested that they be sent information regularly.

Text-based E-MAIL is the simplest form of push, and variants based on the delivery of entire web pages exist, complete with links, graphics and tables. But more complex push applications, which offer all sorts of real-time information delivered via custom software, have not made a lasting impression.

QoS

Quality of Service, a term used to describe the reliability (or otherwise) of a NETWORK, based on an underlying assumption that it can always be improved. QOS is difficult to guarantee on PACKET-SWITCHED networks as the volume of traffic and behaviour of packets is hard to predict, but some kinds of network connection have special facilities that make it easier. Companies using ATM, for example, can choose a level of service that suits their specific requirements. A special PROTOCOL, RSVP, can be used to reserve channels on some networks for use by time-sensitive, high-BAND-WIDTH applications such as video.

QUERY

Any request for information from a DATABASE, used by everything from SEARCH ENGINES to web-based railway timetables. A special language, SQL (Structured Query Language), is often used to construct queries.

58% of new American Internet users are women. At current growth rates, women will outnumber men on the Internet by 60% to 40% by 2002.

QUICKTIME

Apple's software MULTIMEDIA technology. Quicktime is used to add audio and video to websites and other multimedia applications, and is an alternative to STREAMING MEDIA products from Real Networks and MICROSOFT. Despite the fact that versions are available for both Macintosh and WINDOWS PLATFORMS, it is nowhere near as popular as its competitors and is unlikely to be a major player in the Windows market.

R

REALAUDIO

A program for listening to music and other sound across the Internet. RealAudio is the invention of Real Networks, a company founded by Rob Glaser, a former MICROSOFT executive, in 1994. Its great achievement was to allow people to listen to music samples as they were transferred across low-BANDWIDTH connections, rather than having to DOWNLOAD an entire file and listen to it afterwards. RealAudio has since evolved into bigger, better STREAMING MEDIA technologies, including video delivery.

REALNAMES

A commercial system designed to take the pain out of remembering and using URLS. The Real-Names system assigns real, simple words to complex web addresses, so that they can be accessed through a direct NAVIGATION system rather than a hit-and-miss SEARCH ENGINE-based process. For example, if the web address of Acme Plumbing were www.webplumbersinternational.com/usa/montana/acme/contents.html, the company could buy the RealNames KEYWORD Acme and use it to guide potential customers straight to its HOME PAGE from other websites.

One problem with RealNames is that it handles disputes over names in a way guaranteed to enrage potential users. Instead of the first-come, first-served approach used by DOMAIN NAME registrars, RealNames relies on an internal and highly subjective arbitration process to determine who has the right to which name. In the above example a different Acme Plumbing, based in New York, might get the Acme keyword in preference to its Montana-based competitor on the basis that more people are likely to want to visit its site. In cases like this RealNames will assign the name to whichever company or individual it deems more relevant to a browsing customer, even if another company asked for it first and has a perfectly legitimate reason for its use. This process will eventually be handled by an external authority, which may resolve such disputes more effectively.

REGISTRATION AUTHORITY

A company that verifies requests for a digital certificate and authorises the relevant certificate authority to issue it. Such authorities form an essential part of any PUBLIC KEY INFRASTRUCTURE. (See DIGITAL SIGNATURE.)

REGULATION OF INVESTIGATORY POWERS BILL

Legislation proposed by the British government in 2000 that increases its powers of surveillance of electronic communications. The Regulation of Investigatory Powers (RIP) bill has been subject to intense scrutiny by privacy and cyber-rights campaigners, who object to the fact that under the new bill the government will be able to tap all electronic communications completely anonymously. The bill also seeks to allow government agencies to monitor all data traffic, allowing them to see exactly which websites individuals have visited and who they have communicated with, and to obtain copies of PRIVATE KEYS to open encrypted messages and transactions. One further concern is the burden it will impose on ISPs, who may be forced to install costly monitoring equipment at the demand of the home secretary.

REMAILER

An Internet site that allows people to send anonymous E-MAIL. When an e-mail message is sent via a remailer, the remailer removes all the information that might identify the sender, such as name, e-mail address, ISP and IP ADDRESS, before forwarding it to the intended recipient.

Remailers are widely used by contributors to discussions in NEWSGROUPS who wish to remain anonymous for some reason, perhaps to hide personal problems from spouses and bosses or to discuss sensitive religious or political issues without fear of recrimination. Many PORNOGRAPHY distributors also rely on remailers to keep their identities secret, which has led authorities to concentrate on their activities. The most famous remailer, Finland-based ANON.PENET.FI, owned by Johan Helsingius, was subjected to great pressure from several sources, including the Church of Scientology, to reveal the identities of some of its 700,000 users. Police investigations and widespread media coverage followed, at least some of which was hysterical and inaccurate. All this resulted in anon.penet.fi's closure in 1996, but many remailers continue to operate worldwide, and are widely supported by Internet privacy and free-speech campaigners.

REMOTE ACCESS

Access to a computer system or NETWORK from a distant location, usually by dialling in with a MODEM. A typical example of remote access is a dial-up connection to an ISP. Many workers now rely on remote access to stay in touch with their offices while travelling or working at home. By dialling into a remote access SERVER, which is usually equipped with a FIREWALL and other security devices, they can access network resources as if they were on a local machine.

RFC

Request For Comments, one of many numbered documents outlining specifications for proposed Internet standards. Unlike proposals issued by traditional standards bodies such as ANSI (American National Standards Institute) and the ISO (International Standards Organisation), RFCs are generally the work of people or groups working independently. Because of the way it is administered, the RFC approach allows good ideas to be reviewed by the whole Internet COMMUNITY rather than by a select few committee members.

Most of the Internet's most widely used standards and PROTOCOLS have emerged from the RFC process, including IP, HTTP, URLS and the E-MAIL format standard (a full list is maintained by the IETF). Some are rather gnomic (see RFC 124, for example), but others are more expansive; a good example is RFC 1118, also known as the Hitchhiker's Guide to the Internet. Unwary researchers have occasionally been caught out by documents such as RFC 2324, which describes HTCPCP 1.0, a way of controlling coffee pots across Internet connections. It is, of course, dated April 1st 1998.

> *There is coffee all over the world. Increasingly, in a world in which computing is ubiquitous, the computists want to make coffee. Coffee brewing is an art, but the distributed intelligence of the web-connected world transcends art. Thus there is a strong, dark, rich requirement for a protocol designed espressoly for the brewing of coffee. Coffee is brewed using coffee pots. Networked coffee pots require a control protocol if they are to be controlled.*
>
> Extract from RFC 2324

ROT13

A simple ENCRYPTION scheme for text messages, in which each letter of the alphabet is rotated with the one 13 places behind or ahead of it. The sentence "My hovercraft is full of eels" becomes "Zl ubirepensg vf shyy bs rryf" when thus encoded. Some USENET readers and E-MAIL clients include a ROT13 feature, which is often used to avoid offending readers in the more polite NEWSGROUPS or to reveal the secrets of computer games.

ROUTER

A device that decides how and where to send Internet traffic. A router examines the address information carried by each PACKET as it arrives at a NETWORK and chooses the best route to send it to its final destination. Routers maintain their own records of available network pathways and the prevailing traffic conditions to help them decide on the most code-effective routes. Every router must be connected to at least two distinct networks, each running the same set of PROTOCOLS. Network GATEWAYS, POPS and some SWITCHES include routing functions.

RSA

A powerful encryption scheme based on principles of PUBLIC KEY CRYPTOGRAPHY. Developed by

Ron Rivest, Adi Shamir and Leonard Adelman (on whose names the abbreviation is based) at the Massachusetts Institute of Technology (MIT) in 1977, RSA is probably the most widely used security algorithm of its kind. It is included in many commercial products, including those developed by MICROSOFT, NETSCAPE and LOTUS. (See ENCRYPTION.)

The magic words are squeamish ossifrage.
Contents of the message encrypted in the first RSA Challenge, cracked in 1994 after 17 years

RSAC
A system for rating the CONTENT of websites, commonly built into BROWSERS and other ONLINE products. The Recreational Software Advisory Council (RSAC) was originally created to rate computer games, helping parents to shield their children from excessive violence, obscene language and other adult content. In its Internet version, based on the PICS specification, RSAC rates web pages on three different criteria (sex, violence and language). Parents who are worried about children being exposed to violence but open-minded about them looking at naked people can control their access to these things fairly precisely. Despite a promising start in life, RSAC is not as widely used as its creators would like.

RSVP
ReSerVation Protocol, an emerging standard for reserving BANDWIDTH on high-speed networks. RSVP is especially useful in MULTICASTING environments, where the timely delivery of audio and video data is critical. (See also QOS.)

RTFM
Read the ……. manual, a suggestion often directed at NEWBIES asking obvious questions about technical subjects in NEWSGROUPS.

SCRIPT

A simple program or sequence of instructions that is carried out by another program. All sorts of programs use scripts as a way of automating procedures or carrying out simple tasks. Many communications programs, for example, use scripts to control the LOGIN sequence by automatically sending a username and PASSWORD when prompted by the HOST computer.

The most common use of scripts in the web environment is to control web pages, either in the BROWSER or on the SERVER. Scripting languages such as JAVASCRIPT and JScript are designed to slot into standard HTML code and provide features beyond those of the mark-up language itself, such as checking the status of web forms or changing the appearance of some page elements when a button is pressed. The scripts that are written for these functions are interpreted directly by the browser, without any need to pass data back to the server for processing.

Some scripted languages, such as PERL, are specifically designed to run on servers. These are often fully-fledged programming languages, which can do more complex jobs and can interface more ably with other system elements such as DATABASES. Generally, these are also interpreted languages, but they are sometimes compiled to improve performance.

SCRIPT KIDDIE

A pejorative term for an aspiring HACKER or CRACKER, especially one who modifies VIRUSES and other harmful pieces of software with the intention of disrupting other people's computer systems. Script kiddies usually regard themselves as ingenious and daring, but they are generally treated with disdain by hardcore hackers and crackers, who consider them lazy, untalented and incapable of writing real software. Still, they are capable of wreaking considerable havoc. Many contemporary E-MAIL-hosted viruses, including 2000's disruptive I Love You and its variants, are the work of script kiddies, and much of the damage caused by TROJAN HORSE programs has been ascribed to their work.

SDMI

The Secure Digital Music Initiative, a scheme developed by a consortium of music industry heavyweights and technology companies to prevent the piracy of music on the Internet. SDMI aims to counter the threat posed by MP3, a way of recording music from CDs that makes it easy to distribute electronically. It uses ENCRYPTION and watermarking techniques to discourage unauthorised copying and distribution. Many companies have expressed support for SDMI's proposals, including manufacturers of portable music players that can store music in memory rather than on moving disks. Quite how these relationships will work in practice remains to be seen, as many of the companies that have signed up for SDMI are already making money from MP3. Believers in SDMI say that the technological advances in its core components, including new encoding techniques that deliver better sound quality than MP3, will gradually move people away from a format that is some ten years old. But with hundreds of thousands of players already in the market, and millions of MP3 tracks in circulation on the Internet, the sheer momentum of MP3 will be difficult to slow.

The difficulty seems to be, not so much that we publish unduly in view of the extent and variety of present-day interests, but rather that publication has been extended far beyond our present ability to make real use of the record. The summation of human experience is being expanded at a prodigious rate, and the means we use for threading through the consequent maze to the momentary important item is the same as was used in the days of square-rigged ships.
Vannevar Bush, from *As We May Think*, 1945

SEARCH ENGINE
Software that finds things on the Internet, usually

a dedicated website. One way or another, most web users eventually find their way to one of the big names, such as ALTAVISTA or YAHOO, because, though far from perfect, they are the only way of finding information in the vastness of the Internet. The reputation of search engines has been steadily diminishing almost from the day that they first appeared, as it has become clear they are not up to the immense job of indexing the web. A 1999 survey by the NEC Institute, a computer science research organisation, found that the biggest search engine, FAST, indexed only one-quarter of the web's 800m pages. The combined efforts of the 11 leading search engines was only enough to cover 42% of the total.

This apparent shortcoming is not immediately obvious to users, who seem to have the opposite problem: too much information. Even quite complex and detailed searches can yield vast lists of sites, with little guidance available on how useful each is likely to be. Most engines have no useful way of determining the relevance of each occurrence of a word, so they simply list them all according to the frequency with which they occur or how near the top of the document they are. There are variations on this theme. Google, for example, ranks sites according to how many others LINK to them, a good indication of the regard in which they are generally held. But even the best sites suffer from a plethora of broken and outdated links, which is a source of immense frustration for users.

Some of these problems can be solved by increased horsepower and improved application of information theory. Unfortunately, most search engines now focus more on marketing, ADVERTISING and strategic partnerships than on the core technology. Some sell rankings to companies which pay to appear at the top of the search list, raising doubts about their objectivity. Others exclude potentially useful sites on the basis that they are in some way competitive. The overall picture is not encouraging, and many researchers are investigating ways of improving the search process.

SENDMAIL

The UNIX implementation of the SMTP PROTOCOL, used to deliver E-MAIL.

SERVER

A program that provides services to another program, often one running on a different computer. On the Internet the most commonly encountered examples are web servers, which are programs that send HTML pages in response to a request from a client, in this case a BROWSER. Several different types of server software can run on a single computer at the same time. A web server, a DATABASE server and even a game server can theoretically all run on the same machine, although in practice the overheads imposed by each usually make this impractical. The term is also used to refer to a computer running a particular program, especially in the case of a FILE SERVER.

SERVER FARM

A group of computers configured as SERVERS gathered together in a single location. Server farms may be used for several different reasons. A busy website, such as a popular SEARCH ENGINE, may use a server farm to spread the load of user requests across several machines, improving the speed of response and managing data transfers more efficiently. The big search engines have server farms numbering tens or even hundreds of computers. In a company a server farm may consist of a bunch of machines all doing different jobs and perhaps even running different OPERATING SYSTEMS; for example, one handling mail, another providing file and print services and a third being used for back-up purposes.

SERVLET

A small JAVA program that runs on a SERVER; in essence, the server equivalent of an APPLET. Servlets have some advantages compared with similar programs written to the CGI specification, for example, because they can use technical features of the Java VIRTUAL MACHINE to run faster.

Most web servers provide facilities to run servlets.

SET

Secure Electronic Transactions, a collection of software algorithms for enabling the security of financial transactions on the Internet. SET, which is built into popular BROWSERS such as INTERNET EXPLORER and NAVIGATOR, is based on DIGITAL SIGNATURE and certificate technology, using many of the elements of a PUBLIC KEY INFRASTRUCTURE. Each transaction between a buyer, a seller and the buyer's bank is authenticated by the exchange of these signatures and certificates. SET includes software technology from several vendors, including NETSCAPE'S SSL and MICROSOFT'S STT.

SETI@HOME

An initiative to enlist the aid of Internet users in the Search for Extraterrestrial Intelligence. Instead of trying to make sense of the vast amount of information collected by SETI's radio telescopes by running it through the organisation's overtaxed computers, SETI@home parcels out the task to volunteers. Thus distributed across a great many computers, the job of looking for messages from alien civilisations becomes more manageable. A similar approach has been used to crack ENCRYPTION schemes such as DES. Unlike the DES effort, SETI@home has yet to yield positive results, although this is not for the want of trying; over 2m participants signed up for the project in its first year.

SHOCKWAVE

A popular PLUG-IN for web pages, used by designers to add sophisticated MULTIMEDIA features to their sites.

SILVER SURFER

A web-surfing enthusiast of advancing years. Older web users are becoming increasingly interesting to advertisers and retailers. According to a survey by Media Metrix, an American research firm, they constitute the fastest-growing demographic group in the American Internet market, where one-fifth of users are aged between 45 and 64. Many other studies have shown that older people use the web more often, stay ONLINE longer and visit more websites than younger users, making them irresistible to advertisers. They also have more money and own more credit cards, and are thus good targets for sales of everything from high-tech gadgets to cars. E-MAIL is especially popular among silver surfers, and many CHAT systems now include rooms for the over-50s.

SLIP

Serial Line Interface Protocol, a way for computers to connect to the Internet across a MODEM-based link. SLIP is getting a bit long in the tooth and suffers from poor error-handling, making connections potentially unreliable. Its next of kin PPP is now more commonly used for dial-up Internet connections.

SMILEY

See EMOTICON.

SMS

Short Messaging Service, a way for mobile phone users to send each other short text messages from the keypads of their GSM phones. Especially popular with teenagers, SMS is also used by many doctors, salespeople and other professionals as a cheap and easy way of sending and receiving time-critical information. Some companies offer SMS-TO-E-MAIL gateways, allowing subscribers to send and receive Internet e-mail while they are on the road.

SMTP

Simple Mail Transport Protocol, the standard way of transferring E-MAIL from one computer to another on the Internet. ISPs typically maintain an SMTP server to which mail clients must connect when sending messages. SMTP generally works in tandem with mailbox management software based on POP3 or IMAP.

SOURCE CODE

The original code of a computer program. Unlike executable binary code or BYTECODE, which has been turned into the ones and zeros that computer processors can understand, source code can be read by humans, albeit rather specialised ones. The source code of commercial software products has traditionally been jealously guarded by its creators, who fear that competitors may use its secrets to copy their expensive new features. But this has been challenged by the OPEN SOURCE movement.

SPAM

Junk E-MAIL. Spam is a major problem for many Internet users, who find their mailboxes and favourite NEWSGROUPS fill up daily with advertisements for get-rich-quick schemes and pornographic websites. The senders of spam, who are called spammers, collect e-mail addresses from newsgroups, e-mail directories and third-party vendors, to which they then send unsolicited messages. They can also collect them with specially written AGENT software, or generate them automatically with specially written computer programs. Some of these work on the basis that any reasonably sized ISP will have a subscriber called Sean, 26 more called SeanA, SeanB and so on, and many other variations on this theme.

The regulation of spam, like so many other kinds of regulation on the Internet, has proved to be extremely difficult. Some individuals have been banned by dozens of ISPs because of their spamming activities, which include the use of e-mail for cheap political campaigning. USENET, with its thousands of public forums, has been hit particularly hard by spammers, who have been diligent in posting their adverts across dozens or even hundreds of newsgroups. Large ISPs have also suffered. AOL, in particular, has been criticised for its policy of publishing information about subscribers, including hobbies, that makes it easy for spammers to target their e-mails. It also provided limited mail filtering features in early versions of its e-mail client. But AOL is by no means alone, and many e-mail accounts with MSN and other providers have been rendered more or less unusable because of the volume of unwanted mail.

The origin of the name is obscure. Many people agree that it derives from a sketch by Monty Python, a group of British comedians, which features a large number of occurrences of the word "spam" in the script, the credits and a song. A few more literally minded observers have suggested that it stands for Self-Propelled Advertising Material.

SPAMMER

Someone who sends SPAM to people or NEWS-GROUPS.

SPYWARE

Software that conceals itself in other programs and reports back to its creators on their usage. Coined by programming wizard Steve Gibson, the expression was originally used to describe a program that collected non-identifiable user information for ADVERTISING purposes without the user's knowledge, raising the inevitable privacy concerns among web users. Many other programs have since been shown to have spyware characteristics. Some large companies have been severely criticised for collecting data without the user's permission, most notably Real Networks, whose RealJukebox program for recording from CDs on to hard disks reported details of its users' listening habits and music libraries back to corporate headquarters. Recent versions have had this feature removed.

SSL

Secure Sockets Layer, a set of security PROTOCOLS invented by NETSCAPE for protecting electronic financial transactions. SSL is an open specification that includes ENCRYPTION software based on the RSA algorithm. It is an important part of the SET specification.

START-UP

A new business venture, especially in the high-technology area. The start-up culture is especially strong in the United States, where venture capital is more readily available than in Europe and where investors are much more knowledgeable about technology. The situation is changing rapidly elsewhere in the world, as the riches on offer for funding good ideas become more visible, although some highly publicised start-up failures have forced investors to look much more sceptically at new business ideas for the web.

> *There's a term in business school now: "Doing a Google". That means raising a lot of money without having a clear business model.*
> Sergey Brin, co-founder of the Google search engine

STANFORD UNIVERSITY

An academic institution of unrivalled influence in the high-tech world. Many of Silicon Valley's most successful companies were formed by Stanford graduates, including Hewlett-Packard, CISCO, SUN MICROSYSTEMS and YAHOO. Famous alumni include Vint Cerf, so-called father of the Internet, and Jim Clark, founder of NETSCAPE.

STEGANOGRAPHY

The science of communicating in a way that hides the existence of the communication. Unlike codes, which render communications unreadable but nonetheless potentially interceptable, steganography (from a Greek phrase meaning covered writing) relies on hiding messages where they would not be expected.

Steganographic tools such as invisible inks and microdots long have been used by espionage agencies. Now digital versions of these tools are creeping into the Internet culture. Owners of digital images, for example, can encode a watermark within JPEG or GIF files to track pirate copies of their property. A casual observer will see nothing but the picture itself, but the creators of the watermark can detect its pattern. Such techniques are being extended to audio files, and form an important part of the SDMI anti-piracy initiative. Encrypted music samples can be played normally by appropriate hardware or software without the listener being aware of alterations to the signal. The ENCRYPTION cannot be removed without critically damaging the sound quality.

STICKINESS

A highly valued but generally unmeasurable quality of a website that keeps its visitors hanging around or encourages them to come back often. Advertisers like stickiness – and what advertisers like, websites try hard to deliver. Quite how to obtain it is not well established as web audiences are notoriously fickle, but some favoured techniques include adding high-level CONTENT and STREAMING MEDIA samples; running competitions; providing extended features such as CHAT or discussion groups; including games sections or BANNER advertisements including interactive features; and building in lots of LINKS referring to other parts of the same site or group of sites.

STREAMING MEDIA

Audio, video and other CONTENT sequences that can be played as they arrive. Instead of downloading a whole file in one go and then playing it back, streaming media technologies such as those developed by Real Networks and MICROSOFT load the file into a memory buffer. Once a suitably large segment has downloaded (20 seconds worth, say) it starts to play, so viewers or listeners do not have to wait minutes or hours to experience their chosen clip. The makers of such software are adamant that audio and low-resolution video can be streamed efficiently across ordinary 56K dial-up connections to the net, although anyone who has tried the experience will probably think the claims are exaggerated.

There is intense competition in the streaming media market, especially between Real and Microsoft, as more and more companies seek to include television-like features in their ONLINE presences. But its evangelists have not done a good job of explaining how people can make money out of it in its current form. Although the technology is leaping ahead, the business case for using it remains far from clear, except to some companies already in the media business. As BANDWIDTH increases, however, the market for such features will surely grow. A Datamonitor report published in 1999 suggested that video and audio streaming would account for 6% of total Internet traffic by 2003.

STYLE SHEET
A template attached to a web page that describes how it should look. The idea of style sheets was borrowed from early word processors and desktop publishing programs. They are used by designers to apply a consistent look and feel to their sites, by making sure that all headlines appear automatically in the same typefaces and colours, for example, and that all the body text is formatted correctly. The latest version of HTML, version 4, replaces some outdated TAGS with new style sheet information, and the W3C has developed a cascading style sheet (CSS) specification, which it recommends for use when developing new web pages.

SUN MICROSYSTEMS
The creator of JAVA and a major player in the development of new Internet technologies. Founded by a bunch of STANFORD UNIVERSITY graduates, Sun's original strength was as a supplier of high-powered workstations built around its own SPARC microprocessors and running the UNIX operating system. But the company faced a considerable problem in the 1990s as MICROSOFT WINDOWS and Intel chips (known collectively as Wintel) became increasingly dominant and demand for its products slowed. Sun turned to its talented engineers (including Bill Joy, who rewrote one version of Unix to include support for TCP/IP, among other things) to produce a system that could take the bat-

tle back to the Wintel giant. The eventual result was JAVA, a language designed to run on any computer and, by extension, remove people's dependence on WINDOWS and Pentium processors.

Java has been a tremendous success in the programming community and has done a good job of bringing Sun to the attention of the world once more. Whether it can achieve its full potential is not yet clear; in the meantime, Sun has been busy with JINI. It still relies on sales of powerful workstations and servers for the bulk of its revenue.

SWITCH

A NETWORK device that moves data traffic between networks. Switches often incorporate some of the functions of a ROUTER but are generally simpler in operation, making decisions only about the next destination of a piece of data rather than planning complex routes. Most networks on the Internet use PACKET-SWITCHING to move data around, although some, such as those based on ATM, are in part CIRCUIT-SWITCHED. The type of switch determines many of a network's fundamental characteristics and is the cause of much disagreement between BELLHEADS and NETHEADS.

T1

See T-CARRIER.

T-CARRIER

A digital telecommunications system developed by Bell Labs in the 1960s. The most commonly used types of T-carrier connection are T1 and T3 lines. T1 lines, which typically carry data at 1.5MBPS (although speeds of 2Mbps are possible), are commonly used by ISPS to supply corporate BANDWIDTH; 45Mbps T3 lines are also in widespread use. T-carrier systems can use many kinds of transmission media, including TWISTED PAIR copper, coaxial cable, FIBRE OPTIC and even microwave.

In Europe a roughly parallel E-carrier system is used in which an E1 line, which carries data at 2.048Mbps, is equivalent to an American T1. Thereafter the capacity of E-carrier lines is measured in straight multiples of the E1 capacity, so an E2 line has a capacity of 4.096Mbps, an E3 6.144Mbps, and so on.

T3

See T-CARRIER.

TA

See TERMINAL ADAPTER.

TAG

One of the defining elements of the HTML mark-up language in which web pages are written. Tags, which are simple text expressions such as <FONT> or <B>, are used to describe how an element of a web page should look or behave. When a BROWSER loads the page it reads the tags and interprets their instructions accordingly. So a piece of HTML which reads

```
<FONT color=#00AA00 face="arial,
helvetica, geneva, sans serif"
size=3><B>Pocket Internet</B></FONT>
```

will display the words "Pocket Internet" in bold type, the Arial typeface (by first preference) and a fetching shade of green.

The ways in which different browsers interpret tags vary, which is why a page that looks one way in NAVIGATOR may be almost unrecognisable in OPERA. For this and other reasons, many tags (including the <FONT> tag) are facing redundancy in the next version of HTML, which recommends other, more consistent ways of achieving the same effects. (See STYLE SHEET.)

TCP

Short for Transmission Control Protocol, software that manages the transfer of data across a NETWORK. TCP handles the complex job of breaking data up into discrete PACKETS, handing them across to another program to deliver them, making sure they have all arrived at the right destination and then reassembling them in the right order. The delivery part of this process is handled by IP, which is why the two are usually bracketed together. (See TCP/IP.)

TCP/IP

The software that makes the Internet work. It is useful to think of TCP/IP as a kind of electronic removals outfit, which is used to ship data from one physical place to another. The TCP part of the outfit is responsible for the donkey-work of packing everything up individually and labelling it carefully. IP handles the driving of the digital van (or vans, which may all take different routes) and the map-reading. Once everything has arrived at the right address TCP then takes over again, unpacking everything and putting it back in its proper place.

The TCP/IP combination has triumphed over other PROTOCOLS because it works efficiently across disparate networks and many different kinds of computer PLATFORMS. Every major OPERATING SYSTEM now speaks TCP/IP (or can easily be made to); and although some network purists have argued that other alternatives are more robust or more secure, none has been able to find a cheap, fast, easy-to-use way of doing the same jobs.

T

TELEHOUSE

A secure telecommunications facility in London's Docklands. Telehouse is in effect a transit warehouse for the UK's Internet traffic, housing facilities for most of the country's large ISPs and international CARRIERS.

TELNET

A program used to access a remote computer. Some Internet PROTOCOLS such as HTTP allow you to access material on an Internet site anonymously, but telnet requires you to LOGIN to a computer with a username and a PASSWORD. Once logged on, various facilities may be provided by the HOST computer, especially E-MAIL, as if you were actually sitting at the computer itself. Most OPERATING SYSTEMS include a telnet client as a standard part of the furniture. Telnet hosts usually run simple terminal-style, text-only interfaces with arcane command line interfaces, often running on top of variants of the UNIX operating system. Some ISPS provide a telnet interface to their mail SERVER, allowing subscribers to access their e-mail from any machine with a telnet program – that is, nearly all of them.

THIN CLIENT

A stripped-down INFORMATION APPLIANCE used to communicate with a central information source, often used as a synonym for NETWORK COMPUTER. The economic idea behind thin clients is a simple and attractive one: don't pay for features that you don't need. So computers of this kind have no CD-ROM drives, no hard disks and no sound cards. The only software they possess is that needed to connect to the mothership-like SERVER, which provides applications and services as they are required. So far the thinness of such devices has been more or less matched by that of the business being done by their manufacturers.

THREAD

The trail of responses to a message posted in a NEWSGROUP or other electronic forum. Following the thread of a discussion is often difficult when there are many different simultaneous conversations going on, so some newsreaders, E-MAIL clients and server-based discussion software provide a visual means of doing so. Threaded discussions usually appear as a series of hierarchically indented responses to the original message.

3G

Abbreviation for third-generation networks, a generic term for a forthcoming generation of mobile wireless communications systems. 3G networks promise to improve on existing wireless data communications by massively increasing the BANDWIDTH available to small devices such as telephones and PDAs from the typical 9,600bps in use today to 2MBPS, faster than the great majority of today's Internet connections. At such speeds, it will be possible to DOWNLOAD all sorts of things to mobile devices, including video, music and searchable, indexed text, thus transforming them from the comparatively dumb terminals they are today into potentially intelligent information appliances.

Optimistic estimates of 3G rollout suggest that the new networks will replace existing wireless networks within 2–3 years. But the road to 3G is a tortuous one, involving stops at intermediate technologies such as GPRS (general packet radio service) along the way and almost certainly culminating in the usual rash of competing standards. Several other problems exist, particularly for operators of high-bandwidth services, who will have to undergo an expensive transition from voice-based communications companies to data providers. Furthermore, nobody knows how people will want to use this extra bandwidth. It is hard to develop features that people don't yet know they want, and so it is likely that 3G services will experience the same sluggish start as WAP services did.

THUMBNAIL

A small version of a larger IMAGE. Many websites,

especially those with collections of software screen shots or photographs, use thumbnails to display lots of miniaturised versions of their pictures. This speeds DOWNLOAD times and makes it easier for visitors to browse through the goods on offer before committing to a BANDWIDTH-intensive download.

TIGER TEAM

A team of skilled security experts or HACKERS hired to probe a corporate NETWORK for weaknesses and reveal potentially disastrous security holes. Tiger teams resort to a wide variety of tactics to gain access to computer networks and company resources, some of a distinctly low-tech nature. Rifling through dustbins looking for valuable network information, cajoling passwords out of employees by phone, stealing security badges and breaking into vaulted SERVER rooms through the roof are all tried and tested techniques. Nevertheless, their technical exploits are legendary, and some observers have noted that were their exploits made public they would be regarded as some of the most brilliant hacks in the history of computing. Some teams claim 100% success records, neatly demonstrating in the process that the strongest FIREWALLS and ENCRYPTION algorithms are only as tough as the weakest human or physical links.

Tiger teams have existed in the military and commercial worlds for years, being used to test the integrity of everything from banks to nuclear laboratories and weapons plants. Their arrival in the Internet world is an inevitable consequence of the fears about security of E-COMMERCE transactions and privacy of customer information, as well as a certain paranoia among .COMS that some of their less enviable business performance figures might be revealed.

TLA

Three-Letter Acronym, such as IMO (in my opinion). (See ACRONYM.)

TROJAN HORSE

A malicious program or piece of code contained within an apparently harmless program. Trojan horses are often installed inadvertently by people receiving, for example, electronic greetings cards by E-MAIL. Some Trojans simply damage data on hard disks or perform various kinds of mischief, such as displaying odd messages on the computer screen. More sophisticated modern versions can open up a computer to attack from the Internet, allowing a CRACKER or SCRIPT KIDDIE with the right software to effectively take over control of the machine. One famous Trojan horse program, Back Orifice, was created by a HACKER group, Cult of the Dead Cow, to illustrate security holes in MICROSOFT OPERATING SYSTEMS. Other common examples are Netbus and SubSeven. Many anti-VIRUS programs now routinely scan for the well-known Trojans, and some personal FIREWALLS prevent them from advertising their presence to potential intruders.

TRUSTED THIRD PARTY

An organisation entrusted with the keeping of cryptographic keys. The apparent idea behind the appointment of trusted third parties (TTPs) is that by holding a copy of someone's public key they can provide independent confirmation of that person's identity to other parties in an E-COMMERCE deal. This is in itself not a bad idea, but governments are also keen to use TTP schemes to keep tabs on suspected criminals who are using strong cryptography. This process may or may not require a warrant.

Proposed TTP schemes all suffer from major flaws, which render them unusable in practical ways. The most obvious is that the sorts of people governments claim to be targeting with their proposals are unlikely to co-operate with authorities and turn over copies of their PRIVATE KEYS.

Supporters of cryptography point out that law-abiding citizens are at the greatest risk from such KEY ESCROW schemes. In particular, businesses seeking to get involved in e-commerce have had their confidence severely undermined by the looming threat of TTP. Their concerns are many and legitimate. All these schemes are open to abuse by government officials and security organisations, whose records in this area are not unblemished. Moreover, the third parties themselves are almost irresistible targets for malicious CRACKERS, for whom large-scale stores of private keys represent a playground of immense proportions. This inevitably makes TTPs horribly expensive to administer, as they require military-grade security to keep them closed to unauthorised visitors. (See also PUBLIC KEY CRYPTOGRAPHY.)

TTP
See TRUSTED THIRD PARTY above.

TUNNELLING
A technique used to create private networks on the public systems of the Internet. Using tunnelling, companies can build their own VIRTUAL private networks (VPNS) without the need for expensive dedicated systems and LEASED LINES, by encapsulating a separate NETWORK PROTOCOL within standard TCP/IP PACKETS. The IETF is considering several proposals for a standard tunnelling protocol, including PPTP (Point-to-Point Tunnelling Protocol) from MICROSOFT and Layer 2 Forwarding from CISCO.

TWISTED PAIR
The pair of copper wires that connect most people to the Internet. Despite the invention of many newer and glitzier ways of transmitting data between two points, copper wire remains the cheapest and most convenient to use because it is installed in so many homes as part of the ordinary telephone system. Some new high-speed networks, such as those based on DSL technologies, can run happily across copper.

UNIFORM RESOURCE LOCATOR
See URL.

UNIX
An OPERATING SYSTEM, the inspiration behind much modern software and the code on which the Internet was originally built. Invented by Ken Thompson at AT&T's Bell Labs in 1969, the original purpose of Unix was apparently to provide a way for its author to play games on his computer. It quickly turned into an enormously powerful and secure system capable of supporting big networks, and is now used by everyone from small academic institutions to huge ISPS.

This transformation of Unix can be largely ascribed to its continued development and fine-tuning by many different groups of people. AT&T's decision to release the SOURCE CODE to universities ensured that the system influenced lots of up-and-coming computer scientists and developers, whose freedom to tinker with the innards had both good and bad results. On the positive side, Unix has become a flexible and open development environment in which programmers can create powerful programs that do particular jobs extremely well. The prowess of some Unix tools, such as the EMACS text processor, is legendary. So influential was Unix that some of its elements can even be seen in the design of comparatively trivial operating systems such as MICROSOFT'S DOS and WINDOWS.

Less positively, Unix has struggled to shake off its HACKER image and is still too difficult for ordinary folk to use in everyday computing. This has not been helped by the fragmentation of the system into competing flavours. Despite efforts by SUN MICROSYSTEMS, SCO (Santa Cruz Operation, a software company) and others to create friendlier versions of Unix that smooth over its many complexities and inconsistencies, the software has not been widely adopted by companies and has lost a great deal of ground to Microsoft's WINDOWS NT.

A light at the end of the tunnel is LINUX, a cousin of Unix, which has captured the imagination of the business world in a way that mainstream Unix never quite managed. As Sun focuses the bulk of its attention on JAVA and JINI, Linux may yet be the software that keeps the Unix spirit alive and in circulation on the Internet.

UPLOAD

To transfer information from a local computer to a remote one, such as a web SERVER, across a NETWORK or MODEM connection. When transferring files across an Internet connection, the file transfer protocol (FTP) is generally used. Other forms of transfer (to a BULLETIN BOARD, for example) use standard communications protocols like ZMODEM.

URI

Uniform Resource Identifier, a way of locating and finding a specific resource or piece of CONTENT on the Internet, such as a page of text, an IMAGE file or a video sequence. There are several types of URI, of which by far the most important is the URL.

URL

Uniform Resource Locator, an Internet address that describes the location of a specific site or document, usually on the WORLD WIDE WEB. A complete URL describes both the PROTOCOL used by the site in question (HTTP, FTP, GOPHER, and so on) and a DOMAIN NAME (economist.com, for example). A machine name specifying the actual part of the domain where the document resides, such as www, is usually included (although this is not a necessity – many sites do without it). So the complete URL for *The Economist*'s website is:

http://www.economist.com

This simple example is easy for most web users to remember, but most are more complex and would take forever to type even if they were memorable. Several solutions to this problem have been devised. The simplest have been implemented in BROWSERS, which can now remember all the URLs visited in the recent past and even type them in for you. More ambitious is the REAL-NAMES project, which attempts to assign a memorable name to a web address rather than a complex and incomprehensible string of characters. The fly in this otherwise attractive ointment is that it uses an apparently arbitrary way of determining who has the right to which RealName. Like it or not, the unfortunate fact is that the Internet is simply too big to provide memorable addresses for all its constituents.

USENET

Where NEWSGROUPS live. At the end of the 20th century Usenet was home to over 30,000 of these discussion groups, each dedicated to a specific topic and each containing a bewildering range of conversations. All of human life can be found on Usenet, which attracts and repels potential visitors in more or less equal measure.

Usenet is in effect a vast, distributed BULLETIN BOARD system, running mainly on UNIX machines that communicate with each other through standard Internet PROTOCOLS. First devised at the end of the 1970s as a way for computer enthusiasts to share information, Usenet's early growth was completely independent of the WORD WIDE WEB, which it predated by over a decade. In recent years, most of the traffic in the newsgroups has been generated by people with a dial-up Internet connection, who regard it as just another Internet service. This greatly annoys hardcore Usenetters.

Usenet is almost certainly the largest widely available information source in existence, an extraordinary and daunting resource, but it is in danger of becoming unusable. The sheer volume of traffic generated by its millions of users, now measured in multiple gigabytes every day across all the groups, inevitably includes a high proportion of noise. SPAMMERS proliferate, often posting their messages to hundreds of groups at a time, and the quality of debate is generally reckoned to have declined dramatically. The second big threat is CENSORSHIP. Although several well-publicised attempts to remove newsgroups from the feeds of some ISPs have failed, others have succeeded because they have been made covertly. Many universities and colleges now routinely ban some newsgroups, and others are sure to follow.

We've heard that a million monkeys at a million keyboards could produce the Complete Works of Shakespeare*; now, thanks to the Internet, we know this is not true.*
Robert Wilensky

UUENCODE

A technique for encoding BINARY FILES and messages into a form that can be sent via E-MAIL. Because most e-mail systems cannot handle 8-BIT binary files reliably, ATTACHMENTS must be converted into 7-bit text-only form before sending. Many e-mail programs include Uuencode capabilities for doing just this. Like so many other pieces of Internet-related software, Uuencode began life as a UNIX program but has spread rapidly to all the other major OPERATING SYSTEMS. Some general-purpose COMPRESSION utilities such as Winzip can decode UUE files.

vBNS

The Very High Speed Backbone Network Service, a high-speed BACKBONE funded by the National Science Foundation that connects American supercomputer centres. VBNS is the successor to DARPANET and NSFNET, two of the original networks on which the Internet was based.

VBSCRIPT

A program for creating SCRIPTS based on MICROSOFT's Visual Basic programming language. VBSCRIPT is the equivalent of NETSCAPE's JAVASCRIPT, with one significant difference: Javascript works with Microsoft's BROWSER INTERNET EXPLORER, but VBSCRIPT does not work with Netscape's NAVIGATOR. This means that any code written in VBSCRIPT cannot be used by a large proportion of the browsing public. For this reason, the use of VBSCRIPT has so far been limited to INTRANET-based networks running only Internet Explorer.

VERONICA

A program used to find information on the Internet (see GOPHER).

VIDEOCONFERENCING

Long touted as the miracle technology that would bring people closer together without the need for them to meet physically, videoconferencing has yet to make its mark in most industries. However, despite being hamstrung by BANDWIDTH limitations and cultural obstacles, it is still alive and kicking. The Internet currently solves very few of its problems, as PACKET-based networks are generally unsuitable for delivering video reliably. STREAMING MEDIA technologies are also unsuitable for live video content. Despite all this, Internet companies continue to market hardware aimed at the videoconferencing market, especially cameras of the type popularised by C-U-See-Me software in the web's early days.

VIEWSER

A passive recipient of supposedly interactive

CONTENT on websites, broadly analogous to a chatroom LURKER. Rather than registering for products and services or using the free features, viewers simply pass by in the hope of finding something that catches their attention. Converting viewers to users is a big challenge for sites already struggling to maximise the DWELLTIME of their visitors.

VIRTUAL
Describes something that exists in essence or effect, but not in any physical sense. This hackneyed term is often used to describe electronic phenomena, particularly those relating to a COMMUNITY or other kind of relationship. Virtual girlfriends, virtual worlds, virtual bands, virtual tourists, virtual libraries, virtual postcards and virtual seminars are among its many trite uses on the web. One legitimate use is VIRTUAL MACHINE.

VIRTUAL COMMUNITY
See COMMUNITY.

VIRTUAL MACHINE
Software that acts an interpreter for JAVA programs. The virtual machine (or VM) is a critical part of SUN MICROSYSTEMS's strategy to make Java truly portable among different types of computers, because it is the one common factor across all PLATFORMS. Rather than having to understand the specifics of every kind of computer processor, a programmer writes just one version of a program, which is compiled into BYTECODE. This code is then fed to the virtual machine, which translates its instructions into terms the processor understands.

VMS are available for most types of processor/OPERATING SYSTEM combinations, theoretically enabling a Java program to run as advertised on most of the world's new computers. One problem with all of them is that the process of turning bytecode into native processor instructions is extremely labour-intensive. Much of the criticism for Java's sluggish performance on anything but the fastest computers can be laid at the door of poorly implemented VMS, although this situation is improving rapidly, as computers get more powerful.

VIRUS

A self-replicating piece of software designed to cause damage to computers or inconvenience to their users. Historically transmitted by floppy disks, the Internet has greatly increased the threat posed by viruses as it provides a much-improved distribution NETWORK for infected files. Some imaginative virus writers have harnessed the Internet features of business software to create especially awkward and intrusive programs.

A good example is the Melissa virus, which achieved worldwide fame in early 1999 when it forced several companies, including MICROSOFT, to shut down their E-MAIL networks. Unlike many other types of virus, Melissa does not destroy data on a computer's hard disk; instead, it infects Microsoft Word documents with a macro written in Microsoft's Visual Basic language. When a curious recipient opens an infected document which recently arrived as an e-mail ATTACHMENT, the virus copies itself rapidly by hijacking the local Microsoft Outlook-based e-mail system and mailing itself to the first 50 entries it finds in the address book. What starts as a small ripple of outgoing messages quickly becomes an overwhelming flood, severely overloading mail SERVERS and, if traffic is heavy enough, causing them to fail.

Melissa's fame stems in part from prurient interest from newspapers and magazines, intrigued by the list of pornographic websites contained in the infected Word document. Less attention has been paid to the fact that anyone with an up-to-date copy of Microsoft Office (many tens of millions of people) and a modicum of programming talent can write similar viruses without any need for advanced development tools. This has inevitably lead to the creation of other, more dangerous macro-based viruses, including 2000's I Love You, a variation on the Melissa theme, which also destroyed music and graphics files on hard disks. A rash of other such viruses appeared shortly afterwards, most aiming to exploit security holes in the WINDOWS OPERATING SYSTEM in general and Microsoft Outlook in particular.

VM
See VIRTUAL MACHINE.

VOIP
Voice Over IP (see INTERNET TELEPHONY).

VORTAL
A variation on the popular PORTAL theme, in which a website provides access to information related to a specific industry or area of interest. Vortals are springing up in many guises and are widely expected to be hugely profitable. Many adopt an INFOMEDIARY role, bringing buyers and sellers with shared interests together in a single, manageable place.

VPN
Virtual Private Network. VPNS help solve an expensive problem for companies that want to set up their own private data networks. Instead of relying on costly LEASED LINES to build their infrastructure, they use special ENCRYPTION techniques in conjunction with a new TUNNELLING protocol, PPTP, to broadcast data across public communications channels. VPNS generally require the use of specially adapted FIREWALL software to allow the modified PACKETS used by the network to pass in and out of a LOCAL AREA NETWORK.

VRML
Virtual Reality Modelling Language, originally created by Silicon Graphics to describe three-dimensional environments on the web. Like HTML, VRML (pronounced "vur-mal") code is interpreted by the BROWSER (or, often, a specialised PLUG-IN) and turned into a visual scene. The latest version of this 3-D technology, called VRML 97, includes sophisticated features such as animation and sound, aimed at aiding the creation of immersive environments in which people can interact and

communicate easily. Despite this, few websites use it. The web is odd enough already, it seems, without subjecting people to ever more warped views of it.

V.90

The latest in the V series of MODEM standards. V.90 modems can theoretically transmit data downstream (that is, from a remote machine to the one in which the modem is installed) at 56KBPS. What sets them apart from other modems is that downstream data does not need to be modulated; it is instead passed as a bitstream encoded to use nearly all of a typical ISP's 64K digital line capacity.

W3C

The World Wide Web Consortium, a group devoted to the shepherding of new technical standards for the web. Based at the Massachusetts Institute of Technology (MIT) and headed by Tim Berners-Lee (the inventor of HTML and HTTP, and thus of the web itself), the W3C oversees the development of extensions and additions to the underlying languages and technologies currently propping up the web. A good example of what happens when academics are let loose with great technology is its website, at www.w3.org.

WAP

Wireless Application Protocol, a set of specifications that describes how portable wireless devices such as phones and PDAs should access the Internet and communicate with each other. WAP is the first credible attempt to create standards for net access by such devices, and is already supported by telecommunications companies representing over 100m subscribers. Using WAP, anyone should be able to access the web, E-MAIL, USENET and even IRC from a simple phone-like device.

WAP uses its own local communications mechanisms but is designed to work closely with existing Internet standards, speaking fluently to web transport protocols such as HTTP and TCP/IP and reading many kinds of web content. In the short term, high-BANDWIDTH CONTENT such as video will be beyond WAP's reach, although rapid advances in wireless communications may make this a reality by 2001. But personal banking, timetables, cinema and restaurant bookings and so on are all within WAP's reach.

The first WAP phones were launched with great fanfares in Europe in early 2000, offering access to basic news and other information. Immediately, one of WAP's drawbacks, the cost of developing genuinely useful services, became apparent, and only a handful of companies had launched products by the middle of the year.

W

WAREZ

Pirated software, generally distributed on USENET.
The warez (pronounced wares) movement perfectly exemplifies the difficulties of regulating
Internet activity. Every day many hundreds of
MEGABYTES of illegally copied software are
uploaded to special NEWSGROUPS, from which anyone with an Internet account can then DOWNLOAD
it. The pirates themselves are anonymous and
untraceable, as are the people who download the
software. The elaborate copy-protection mechanisms used by the software's creators are no
match for experienced warez CRACKERS, who routinely break them in days or even hours. A complex form of NETIQUETTE exists among serious
warez traders: anyone regularly downloading software is expected to UPLOAD samples of their own.

WDM

Wave-Division Multiplexing (see MULTIPLEXING).

WEB

The common name for the WORLD WIDE WEB.

WEBCAM

A camera hooked up to the WORLD WIDE WEB showing regularly updated pictures of the subject in
focus. People have pointed Webcams at all sorts
of unusual things, including Coke machines, fish-
tanks, Antarctica, busy traffic routes and, most
intriguingly, themselves. Jennifer Ringley, in particular, has achieved worldwide fame with her
Jennicam, which allows high-tech voyeurs to spy
on her going about her unremarkable daily business. The prospect of watching her do this without any clothes on, a rare but nonetheless
recorded event, is apparently enticing enough to
persuade thousands of people to pay her $15 a
year for the privilege. Anyone seeking to duplicate
her achievement can buy a suitable camera
around $150, but they should consider that the
cost of a permanent connection to the Internet is
not trivial in many places. The amount of traffic
needed to become profitable is substantial, which

is why (Jennifer aside) the only businesses making real money from Webcams are PORNOGRAPHY sites.

WEBCAST

An audio or video broadcast on the web, usually of an event such as a concert, an interview or a sports fixture. Webcasting has become a popular way of increasing the STICKINESS of PORTAL sites, especially those run by ISPs, but it is widely used by traditional media as a way of disseminating material to a global audience. The recent improvement in STREAMING MEDIA technology has given webcasting some much-needed credibility with consumers, but it needs big increases in BANDWIDTH to become really effective. The use of MULTICASTING technology is becoming more widespread for webcast events on the MBONE. Some people use the term to describe PUSH MEDIA.

WEB FARM

See SERVER FARM.

WEBLOG

A website which records and analyses events, usually about a particular subject or containing items with a common theme. In their simplest forms weblogs are not much more than ONLINE diaries of individual activities or ideas, but as their scope broadens they can become considerably more interesting and useful. Good weblogs become detailed and fascinating chronicles of their chosen subject, and typically include articles or analysis written by the website owner, links to and comments on other websites and extensive contributions by the community of visitors to the site. Some weblogs have become notoriously rich and complex resources. One good example is Slashdot, a site devoted to the discussion of many technical subjects and noted for its LINUX coverage.

WEBMASTER

Someone who builds, manages or administers a website. Webmasters are much in demand, although definitions of what they do vary somewhat. In some organisations a Webmaster is broadly the equivalent of a TV or radio producer and has a largely organisational or marketing function, whereas in others he or she may be configuring SERVERS, writing code and designing logos.

> *How many webmasters does it take*
> *to change a lightbulb?*
> *404 (Not found).*

WEB RING

A system for connecting together websites relating to a common theme or subject of interest. Web rings let visitors jump from one site to the next automatically, eventually ending up back where they started, although they can also choose to visits its participating sites randomly. Such rings are popular with web surfers, because unlike SEARCH ENGINES and directories they more or less ensure that the information they contain is relevant to a particular user's sphere of interest. They are also of increasing interest to site owners and advertisers, who see much potential in a self-selecting user base of this kind. The concept was pioneered in 1995 by 17-year-old Sage Weil, who now oversees www.webring.org, the web's biggest collection of rings – over 80,000 in mid-2000, consisting of over 1.3m individual sites. Web rings exist for every conceivable subject of interest to human beings, and some that many people may find inconceivable too. Someone who manages a web ring is known as a ringmaster.

WEBSITE

A location on the WORLD WIDE WEB, identified by a web address such as www.economist.com. Websites consist of one or more pages of information and data encoded with HYPERTEXT MARK-UP LANGUAGE to make them readable by a web BROWSER. Some websites consist of a single home page belonging to an individual or a small company; big corporate sites may consist of thousands of pages. However large or small, it is now considered obligatory for businesses to have a website so as to retain credibility with an increasingly web-conscious customer base.

WEBTONE

Broadly, a Utopian Web equivalent of dialtone: continuous, reliable, round-the-clock access to the Internet. SUN MICROSYSTEMS's definition specifies that Webtone is always "on", like the telephone; that it provides services to business and consumers via a web-based NETWORK; and that it is available to a wide array of devices such as phones, PDAs and perhaps even kitchen implements, such as microwave ovens, at any time. Of these three stipulations, only the first is currently a reality, and then only to those who subscribe to an always-on service such as ADSL.

WEBTV

A service incorporating access to both television and the Internet. Founded by three ex-Apple employees and now owned by MICROSOFT, WebTV was the first company to try to provide these two seemingly incompatible services in one place. It uses a special set-top box (made by licensees such as Philips and Sony) to integrate the functions of an existing television set and a dial-up Internet connection, and can even display both at the same time. There are currently over 500,000 WebTV subscribers in the United States. (See also CONVERGENCE.)

WELL

Short for Whole Earth 'Lectronic Link. The Well was one of the first VIRTUAL communities, and it has built up a mythology of its own since its inception as a mutual support system for hippie commune founders. It is particularly noted for the quality of its debate and discussion, although its loftiness – said by some to be elitism in action – is not easily digested by everyone. Its value to the wider Internet COMMUNITY is now mostly symbolic, although several members of the original Well community maintain a high profile in net cultural circles.

W

WHOIS

A program that tells you the owner of any second-level DOMAIN NAME. Whois programs run either on a web SERVER or from a local machine and provide a quick way of finding out how to contact the owners of a website. Commercial organisations that register domain names provide whois GATEWAYS to determine whether or not a given domain is still available for sale.

WINDOWS

The word's most widely used software, MICROSOFT's Windows product started life in the mid-1980s as an unpromising competitor to Apple's Macintosh OPERATING SYSTEM. Designed principally as a glamorous front-end for its famously lucrative DOS, Windows failed to catch on until its third iteration appeared in 1990. A major cosmetic overhaul and some internal wizardry, which made it easier to install and configure, helped boost its popularity, but the real selling point was the huge amount of third-party software that Microsoft had persuaded people to write. Almost overnight the industry adopted Windows 3.0 and its successor, 3.1, as the new standard around which software was constructed, killing off IBM's competing OS/2 and severely damaging the MacOS in the process.

With no serious competition Windows has grown ever stronger. Recent end-user incarnations, Windows 95 and Windows 98, are easier and safer to use than their predecessors (although still fundamentally flawed, according to many observers). Nearly all commercial software is now written for the Windows PLATFORM. The biggest strides forward have been made in Internet connectivity, which has been included in various forms since 1995. In particular, the addition of the INTERNET EXPLORER BROWSER to the standard Windows package has dramatically altered the Internet landscape. With this unmatchable distribution mechanism, Microsoft has wrested the lion's share of the browser market from NETSCAPE.

Windows itself is still mutating rapidly and is

gradually spreading to every device capable of hosting an operating system, whether it needs one or not. A cut-down version, Windows CE, is widely used in PDAS, and new versions are planned for set-top boxes, smart cards and eventually even fridges and cookers, thus fulfilling Bill Gates's "Windows Everywhere" promise from the early 1990s.

WINDOWS NT

A heavyweight version of MICROSOFT WINDOWS, designed for use in environments where security, fault tolerance and sheer processing horsepower are more important than elegance and speed. Windows NT has supplanted NETWARE and UNIX as the SERVER OPERATING SYSTEM of choice in the corporate world, being generally easier to install and configure. Its critics have attacked its comparatively poor security record, inadequate support for multiple processors and much else besides, but this has not stopped NT's march into territory previously commanded by Netware and Unix. Now installed on many of the world's web servers, it constitutes the supporting layer for Microsoft's E-COMMERCE and web hosting products.

WINDOWS 2000

The latest version of WINDOWS, based on MICROSOFT's NT technology. Windows 2000 was originally designed to replace and unify the many current versions of Microsoft's OPERATING SYSTEM in a single product that would run on desktops, SERVERS and many other smaller devices. But the technical challenges of this amalgamation proved too hard for Microsoft's engineers to solve, and Windows 2000 is effectively the latest version of WINDOWS NT, albeit a considerably more robust and Internet-savvy one. Designed principally for the corporate world, it includes many new features designed to help companies expand and build upon their Internet presences, including web servers and directory services.

WML

Short for Wireless Mark-up Language, which allows text-based web information to be displayed on wireless devices such as mobile phones and PDAs. WML uses existing protocols such as GSM as its transport mechanism and is part of the WAP specification.

Every now and then, a technology or an idea comes along that is so profound, so powerful, so universal that its impact changes everything. The printing press. The incandescent light. The automobile. Manned flight. It doesn't happen often, but when it does, the world is changed forever.

Lou Gerstner, chairman of IBM

WORLD WIDE WEB

The hypermedia technology that makes the Internet usable by mere humans. The World Wide Web, or the web as it is now commonly known, was originally designed to help workers at CERN, the European particle physics laboratory near Geneva, share information among themselves using a single, unified interface. Soon the world realised that the web was of great importance not just to high-energy physicists but to people in almost every other sphere of human activity. The web's subsequent growth can only be described as explosive. In mid-1993, when the first graphical web BROWSER was launched, there were about 150 websites holding a few thousand web pages; at the beginning of 1995 there were about 10,000 sites, a number that grew to 4.5m by mid-1999. In April 2000 it was estimated that over 4,400 new sites were appearing every day.

The technology underlying the web has not changed much since Tim Berners-Lee, often described as the father of the web, outlined the first schemas for HTML and HTTP, the two fundamental building blocks of web technology. What has changed is people's ability to think of new things to do with it. In conjunction with other technology such as JAVA and DHTML, web pages have evolved from mere repositories for static information into busy, interactive environments where people can shop for gifts, exchange goods and services, watch films, learn French and communicate with friends or strangers. It may not yet be the "embodiment of human knowledge" envisaged by Berners-Lee, but at more than 1 billion pages it is getting there fast.

WWW
Short for WORLD WIDE WEB.

XANADU

An ambitious electronic data storage and retrieval
system devised by Theodore Nelson in the 1960s,
named after the mythical place in Coleridge's
poem "Kubla Khan". Nelson is credited with coin-
ing the term HYPERTEXT to help describe his system,
which he portrayed as "a universal instantaneous
hypertext publishing network". Many of Xanadu's
proposed features precede similar ones found in
today's WORLD WIDE WEB, although it is a mistake to
think of Xanadu as being web-like in any mean-
ingful way; indeed, Nelson has been hypercritical
of the web and modern software design generally.
Instead, it concentrates on solving the problems of
version management and rights management
(both serious problems on the web) through the
use of reusable but nonetheless COPYRIGHT hypermedia published from a central pool of CONTENT.

Nelson himself described Xanadu as being well
known but poorly understood, a situation that
was not improved by his tortuous descriptions of
his work and his penchant for contrived words
such as humber (a contraction of humungous
number), xanalogical storage and the DOCUVERSE.
No real implementation of Xanadu exists today,
despite decades of effort by Nelson to realise his
vision, although some of the underlying code was
made available to the OPEN SOURCE COMMUNITY in
1999.

XHTML

Extensible Hypertext Mark-up Language, effectively the latest version of HTML 4.0, the language
used to describe web pages, which has been
reformulated to include elements of XML. As its
name suggests, XHTML's capabilities can be
extended with the addition of new TAGS reflecting
the use being made of the code, so web authors
can customise sites and the way in which their
CONTENT is managed without being hampered by
the restrictions of plain HTML. XHTML also encourages a more structured way of thinking about content, helping WEBMASTERS to manage large or
complex sites more efficiently.

XML

Extensible Mark-up Language, a way of describing and sharing data on networks. Like its cousin HTML, XML consists of a set of TAGS that describe a chunk of data. The resemblance more or less ends there. XML is designed to describe the CONTENT of a page in terms of the type of data it contains, rather than the way that data should look. So while an HTML tag such as <FONT> simply specifies that the following text should be displayed in a particular size and weight, an XML <FISH> tag might indicate that the following data describes a particular species of fish.

This characteristic of XML makes it easy for like-minded groups of people to share information, because they need only agree on a set of tags that meets their particular needs. Thus a global consortium of fishmongers might agree on a standard way of describing information about fish catches – the number landed, the average size of the fish, the different species – and use their own XML tags to actually store the data. An intelligent SEARCH ENGINE could then look for data types rather than just words: all the fishmongers who landed haddock of a particular size on a specified date, rather than just any website containing the word haddock.

Some implementations of XML are already in use. MICROSOFT's Channel Definition Format (CDF), for example, which describes how broadcast-like data channels should be interpreted by BROWSERS, is based on XML. But the language's real importance in the future is in BUSINESS-TO-BUSINESS E-COMMERCE, where its ability to help companies share information will make the automation of many business processes much easier. Several commercial products and strategies, such as Microsoft's BizTalk, are based on XML.

XSL

Extensible Style-sheet Language, which tells a browser how XML TAGS should look. XSL-based STYLE SHEETS are associated with specific XML documents to control the formatting of user-defined tags. XSL can specify where on a page XML data should be displayed and what sort of font it should use, for example. It is based on several other style sheet standards, including the w3c's css.

X.400

A set of standards describing how E-MAIL should be delivered. X.400 is an alternative to SMTP, and is generally more capable but harder to understand and use. One of its drawbacks is the complexity of its addressing format, which is much more difficult to construct than the standard someone@ somewhere.com form used by SMTP.

X.500

Another complex standard, this time for managing directories of people, either on the WORLD WIDE WEB or on private networks. A company can publish an X.500 directory and make it globally available to anyone with Internet access. One of X.500's strengths is its compatibility with other Internet directory and DATABASE standards such as LDAP, WHOIS and FINGER.

Y

YAHOO

A directory of websites, founded by STANFORD UNIVERSITY graduates David Filo and Jerry Yang in 1994. It started life as a simple collection of their own BOOKMARKS, and rapidly grew to become the massive resource it is today, with hundreds of thousands of sites and millions of pages. Yahoo organises the web by category rather than search KEYWORD, using teams of editors to sift through sites and put them in the appropriate boxes. The success of its approach is reflected in the phenomenal traffic it generates; by the end of 1999 Yahoo's website was generating over 300m page views every day. Much of its traffic comes from people attracted by the PORTAL facilities on offer, including CHAT, E-MAIL and AUCTIONS.

In contrast to many Internet companies, Yahoo is notable for its consistent trading in the black. Its multitude of ADVERTISING and promotional deals has generated a revenue stream that competitors such as Excite and LYCOS have struggled to match. The company was highly acquisitive in 1999, successfully completing the purchase of the GEOCITIES ONLINE COMMUNITY and pursuing a buyout of broadcast.com, an aggregator of CONTENT based on STREAMING MEDIA. Filo and Yang are also unusual in that they have managed to retain substantial stakes in the company they founded, and their combined worth is regularly measured in billions of dollars. Nevertheless, like all other Internet companies Yahoo's value has fluctuated dramatically.

70% of the global web population visits just 4,500 sites.

ZAPATA

A fish-oil manufacturer noted for its attempt to become a major Internet player. Avram Glazer, Zapata's chief executive, attracted much derision in 1998 when he made a takeover bid for the Excite SEARCH ENGINE. Shrewder observers subsequently pointed out that with cash reserves of over $100m, Zapata and its Internet arm Zap.com were in a substantially better position to do so than most NEW MEDIA companies and considerably wealthier than Excite itself. Nonetheless, Glazer's attempt came to naught. Despite much blustering about becoming the biggest Internet company in the world, Zap.com remains directionless despite a brief but frantic period of acquisitions in 1998.

ZIP

A popular type of COMPRESSION, used to shrink PC files before transmission across a NETWORK or storage on disk. Many utilities for creating zip files exist, and they are a commonly used format for distributing software on the Internet.

Finland has the world's highest number of Internet users per head: 244.5 per thousand people.

ZMODEM

An error-correcting file transfer PROTOCOL, once widely used by PC communications software but now consigned to a life of leisure on the world's BULLETIN BOARD systems. Zmodem is considerably more efficient than its cousins Xmodem and Ymodem.

ALPHABET ODDBALLS
For entries on **1.0**, **3G** and **404 NOT FOUND** see pages 146, 185 and 88.

Part 3

APPENDICES

1 A brief history of the Internet

Before the beginning

1866 The first fully functional telephone cable is laid across the Atlantic, demonstrating the possibility of rapid communications between continents. Queen Victoria and President Johnson exchange messages across the cable.

1943 Alan Turing builds Colossus, the machine used to decipher German communications in the second world war, and one of the world's earliest programmable electronic computers.

1945 In a highly prescient article in the *The Atlantic Monthly*, entitled "As We May Think", Vannevar Bush, the first director of what eventually became the National Science Foundation, describes a machine he calls a memex. The microfilm-based memex would enable the user to link related pieces of information together for rapid retrieval. Almost 50 years before the web, the ideas were there.

1948 Claude Shannon, a mathematician at AT&T's Bell Labs, publishes *A Mathematical Theory of Communication*. His theory enables the calculation of the information-carrying capacity of any channel. Shannon's work, which included the introduction of the word "bit" to describe a piece of binary information, underpins all information theory and all modern communications systems, including the Internet.

1958 Responding to the launch of Sputnik, the first Earth-orbiting satellite, President Dwight D. Eisenhower creates the Advanced Research Projects Agency (ARPA) to oversee the development of space and military programs. ARPA's brief includes the creation of new computer and communications systems.

1960 J.C.R. Licklider, a researcher at the

Massachusetts Institute of Technology (MIT), publishes "Man-Computer Symbiosis", a paper describing ways in which men and machines might co-operate to make decisions and save valuable time in solving problems.

1961 Leonard Kleinrock, a researcher at MIT, publishes the first paper on packet-switching theory, alerting ARPA scientists to the possibility of treating communications links in terms of passing active packages of information around rather than shovelling them through fixed circuits.

1962 Paul Baran, a computer scientist at the Rand Corporation working on the survivability of communications networks under nuclear attack, describes a distributed computer network for the fist time. His model, in which a network is built of a number of nodes, was revolutionary in its use of messages split up into blocks, each taking a different path to its final destination – in essence, a packet-based network.

1965 The word "packet" is used for the first time by Donald Davies, a British reseacher at the National Physical Laboratory (NPL), to describe a way of breaking up messages for transmission across new kinds of networks. Davies's work mirrored closely that of Paul Baran, although it focused on public communications networks rather military ones.

ARPA sponsors its first study of co-operatively networked computers, involving the connection of two machines in California and Massachusetts across a dedicated 2,000 bits per second telephone link.

Ted Nelson coins the term "hypertext".

1967 Larry Roberts, a computer scientist at ARPA, proposes a design for a fast, decentralised network built on dial-up telephone lines. In London, Donald Davies builds the

National Physical Laboratory Data Network, an early experiment in packet-switching.

At the Association for Computing Machinery Symposium in October, Roberts presents the first paper on the proposed design for the "ARPA net" network.

Representatives of the three bodies researching packet networks (ARPA, RAND and NPL) meet for the first time.

1968 The contract to build the Interface Message Processors (IMPS) at at the core of the experimental ARPA network is awarded to Bolt, Beranek and Newman (BBN), a technical consulting firm in Cambridge, Massachusetts.

The Arpanet age

1969 The first four ARPA network hosts, located at Stanford University, the University of California at Los Angeles (UCLA), the University of California at Santa Barbara and the University of Utah, are connected across 50kbps lines provided by AT&T. The first recorded network crash occurs in October, as the letter G of LOGIN is entered when trying to access the Stanford computer from UCLA.

At Bell Labs, Ken Thompson and Dennis Ritchie invent Unix, the operating system destined to become the bedrock of the Internet.

Compuserve starts life as a computer time-sharing service at an American insurance company.

Telnet, a program allowing people to log into and control computers from a remote terminal, is born.

1970 AlohaNet, a system for exchanging data between computers on four Hawaiian islands, is created by Norman Abramson.

1972 BBN's Ray Tomlinson writes the first e-mail program, and establishes the use of the @ sign in e-mail addresses. In July, Larry

Roberts creates the first program which can list, forward and reply to messages – the first real e-mail client.

The first public demonstration of the ARPA network is held at the International Conference on Computer Communications in Washington's Hilton Hotel; 40 machines take part.

1973 The ARPA network goes global, connecting machines in the United States to hosts at University College in London and The Royal Radar Establishment in Norway.

At Harvard, a PhD student, Bob Metcalfe, outlines the idea for Ethernet, a new and fast way of networking computers. His invention is tested for the first time on computers at Xerox PARC in Palo Alto, California.

1974 BBN launches Telenet, the first commercial packet-switched networking service. Vint Cerf and Bob Kahn publish the first specifications for their Transmission Control Protocol (TCP), a new way of managing the transmission of data packets across networks.

1975 Microsoft is founded by Bill Gates and Paul Allen to produce software for microcomputers. TCP's capabilities are tested across satellite links from the United States to Hawaii and the UK. The first mailing list, MsgGroup, is born on Arpanet.

1976 Queen Elizabeth II sends the first royal e-mail from the Royal Signals and Radar Establishment at Malvern in the UK.

At Bell Labs, researchers develop the Unix-to-Unix Copy program, which later forms the basis of Usenet.

Whitfield Diffie, a cryptographer and privacy advocate, and Martin Hellman, an electrical engineer, invent public-key cryptography.

1977 Three researchers at MIT, Ron Rivest, Adi Shamir and Len Adleman, invent the RSA algorithm (the abbreviation is based on their names), a public key method for encrypting messages.

1978 The TCP protocol is split into two parts, creating the new Internet Protocol (IP). Networks that make use of this protocol become known as internets; the aggregate of these internets constitutes the wider Internet.

1979 Usenet is founded by Tom Truscott and Jim Ellis at Duke University and Steve Bellovin at the University of North Carolina.

Emoticons, also known as smileys, are used for the first time on the Arpanet MsgGroup mailing list.

Richard Bartle and Roy Trubshaw, of the University of Essex in England, create the first multiuser dungeon software for role-playing games.

1981 IBM launches the first personal computer (PC), reshaping the computing landscape. It is equipped with Microsoft's DOS operating system, the source of the company's early fortunes.

The National Science Foundation (NSF) builds the CSNET backbone, a new network for use by academics and researchers with no access to Arpanet.

The Internet age

1982 EUNet, the European Unix Network, is created to provide e-mail and Usenet services between the UK, Denmark, Sweden and the Netherlands.

The Domain Name System (DNS) is established at the University of Wisconsin, bringing order to the previously chaotic addressing system on electronic networks. JANET, the UK's Joint Academic Network, is established.

Widespread development of PC-based local area networks begins.

1983 TCP/IP is officially adopted by ARPA and the

US Department of Defense as the core Internet protocol.

1984 The term "cyberspace" first appears in William Gibson's novel *Neuromancer*.

The Well, one of the net's most famous communities, is started by Stewart Brand, Larry Brilliant and others. It quickly becomes an important forum for electronic discussion.

The first Macintosh computer appears.

1985 The NSF builds on its CSNET idea with the creation of NSFNET, a new high-speed backbone connecting five supercomputing centres in the United States. The arrival of NSFNET triggers an explosion of smaller networks.

America Online (AOL) begins life as Quantum Computer Services.

1986 The Internet Engineering Task Force (IETF) is created to co-ordinate technical developments on Arpanet and key Internet gateway systems.

NNTP, the Network News Transport Protocol, arrives and begins to replace UUCP on Usenet as the standard way of exchanging newsgroup data.

1987 UUNET, a commercial organisation providing access to Usenet and other network services, is founded.

Bill Atkinson writes Hypercard for the Apple Macintosh, the first tool for creating mass-market hypertext and hypermedia applications.

1988 Robert Morris, a computer science graduate at Cornell University, releases a self-replicating program on to the Internet. This so-called worm eventually brings down 6,000 hosts, 10% of all the machines on the network.

Internet relay chat (IRC) is developed in Finland by Jarkko Oikarinen.

1989 In Germany, the Fraunhofer Institute patents the MP3 music compression algorithm.

The World (world.std.com), the first

dial-up Internet Service Provider (ISP), is founded in Massachusetts.

1990 Arpanet officially ceases to be a research tool and becomes just another network.

In July, John Perry Barlow and Mitch Kapor found the Electronic Freedom Foundation (EFF).

1991 A team at CERN, Europe's particle physics laboratory, releases the first text-only "browser" for use with the HTML mark-up language and HTTP protocol that it has developed to allow far-flung researchers to collaborate. Tim Berners-Lee later posts the first public web software on the alt.hypertext newsgroup.

Linus Torvalds, a Finnish student, starts work on writing the operating system that will eventually become Linux.

The first version of Pretty Good Privacy (PGP), a software package that uses the RSA algorithm for encrypting the contents of messages, is released by Phil Zimmerman.

Commercial traffic is permitted to use the NSFNET backbone for the first time. By March, traffic passes 1 trillion bytes and 10 billion packets per month.

Gopher, a program for finding information of the web, is released by the University of Minnesota.

1992 CERN releases its World Wide Web software into the public domain.

The number of Internet hosts passes 1m.

The web age

1993 The first graphical browser, Mosaic for X, written by Marc Andreessen, is released by the National Centre for Supercomputing Applications (NCSA). Traffic on the World Wide Web expands by over 300,000%; by contrast, Gopher usage grows at a mere 997%.

InterNIC is created by the National Science Foundation to direct the management of Internet registration services.

CERN announces that the web and its supporting technology will be freely available to all.

1994 Marc Andreessen and Jim Clark start Netscape, releasing the first version of the Navigator browser in the autumn. Linus Torvalds unveils version 1.0 of the Linux kernel.

The World Wide Web Consortium is formed to steer the development of web technologies, with Tim Berners-Lee appointed as its director.

Laurence Canter and Martha Siegel, two American lawyers, become the most despised people in Internet history after flooding Usenet with advertisements for their green card lottery services, thus becoming the first spammers.

Pizza Hut starts taking orders over the Internet. The first Internet bank, First Virtual, opens in the United States. Wasting no time, Vladimir Levin, a Russian computer expert, becomes the first Internet bank robber, stealing millions of dollars from Citibank.

Traffic on the NSFNET backbone exceeds 10 trillion bytes per month.

1995 The web constitutes the bulk of Internet traffic. Sun Microsystems unveils Java. The first version of the RealAudio audio streaming product appears. Compuserve and AOL, hitherto proprietary networks, provide dial-up access to the Internet for the first time.

Netscape goes public after only 14 months of existence, offering 5m shares to the public on August 8th at an initial price of $28. Shares close at $58.25, valuing the company at over $2 billion and earning its co-founder, Jim Clark, $663m on the first day of trading. In December the share price hits $170.

Jeff Bezos opens his online bookstore at

Amazon.com. The web-based eBay auction house accepts its first bids.

Digital launches its AltaVista search engine, the first serious attempt to index the web.

Microsoft releases Windows 95, the long-awaited upgrade to its popular Windows program. The first version of the company's web browser, Internet Explorer, is released; based on code licensed from Spyglass, it is sold as part of an add-on package for Windows 95.

NSFNET announces that it will no longer provide direct access to its backbone, farming out responsibility for managing access to private companies. Charging for domain names begins, with each costing $50 per year.

Compuserve removes access to 200 pornographic newsgroups after pressure from Bavarian government officials, attracting the ire of free-speech campaigners and anti-censorship activists.

1996 The browser wars begin in earnest as both Microsoft and Netscape each launch the third version of their browsers.

Despite widespread opposition the controversial US Communications Decency Act (CDA), designed to control the distribution of indecent material over the Internet, becomes law in the United States.

Internet telephony, already years old, comes to the attention of American telecommunications companies. America's Carriers Telecommunication Association (ACTA) files a petition to the Federal Communications Commission (FCC) seeking to ban IP telephony products, arguing that they should be subject to regulation. The FCC disagrees.

1997 NASA's home page generates 46m hits in one day as people log in to watch the broadcast from the Pathfinder spacecraft on Mars.

.com and .net addresses disappear for

several hours as human error at Network Solutions causes the DNS table for .com and .net domains to become corrupted, making millions of systems unreachable.

The DES private key encryption system is broken by a collaborative effort between thousands of Internet users, after testing 18 quadrillion possible key combinations. The challenge, set by RSA Data Security, was to decrypt a message which was eventually found to read "Strong cryptography makes the world a safer place".

The Communications Decency Act is overturned by the US Supreme Court, which pronounces it unconstitutional.

Netscape launches version 4 of its browser just ahead of Microsoft. The US Justice Department files its first complaint against Microsoft, on grounds of breaching anti-trust regulations with its browser distribution strategy.

1998 Netscape announces that it will give away not only its browser but the browser's source code as well, an unprecedented move by a software company. A separate division, Mozilla.org, is set up to create products based on the open source element of the business.

Network Solutions registers its 2-millionth domain.

The Microsoft anti-trust trial begins in October. Originally predicted to last eight weeks, the proceedings continue into 1999 as the scope of the trial expands to cover Microsoft's broader exclusionary practices.

AOL and Netscape announce their intention to merge in a $4.2 billion deal, a move seen as a betrayal of Netscape's ideals by web purists. Many Netscape employees resign.

The first portable MP3 players arrive, enabling people to play back pirated digital music. The Secure Digital Music Initiative, designed to prevent this kind of music piracy, is announced by a consortium of music and technology companies.

Portals become big business on the web. Major search engines and ISPs re-engineer their sites to add customisation, chat and auction features.

1999 Day traders operating from home PCs seize opportunities to capitalise on the boom in Internet and other stocks. Charles Schwab, an American stockbroker specialising in electronic trading, sees its market capitalisation rise to $25.5 billion at the end of the financial year, valuing it more highly than many old-style brokers such as Merrill Lynch.

The Melissa virus, carried in Microsoft Word documents, attacks e-mail networks all over the world, replicating itself in enormous numbers and swamping mail servers.

AOL and Microsoft come to blows over chat software, as AOL tries to prevent users of Microsoft's product accessing its huge user base. Microsoft pushes for open standards in the chat market.

Microsoft's web-based e-mail service, Hotmail, is cracked, leaving its 40 million accounts open to access without the need of a password.

In November, Judge Thomas Penfield Jackson rules that Microsoft harmed consumer interests and distorted competition in Internet markets, fuelling speculation about the future of the company and its strategy.

The number of Internet users passes 200 million.

2000 AOL announces a $150 billion takeover of entertainment giant Time Warner, creating the world's biggest media company and gaining access to over 100m subscribers.

The Iridium global satellite communications network goes into liquidation after its failure to turn a $5 billion investment into a viable business. Plans are made to pull the company's 66 satellites out of orbit.

Some of the world's biggest websites, including Yahoo, Amazon and eBay, suffer denial-of-service attacks by malicious hackers, forcing them offline for several hours and renewing concerns about the security of Internet businesses.

The UK's Queen Elizabeth becomes the first royal dot-com millionaire following an investment in Getmapping.com, a site reproducing the *Domesday Book* with digital aerial photographs.

AT&T's wireless communications division raises $10.6 billion on the first day of public trading of its shares, setting a record for the biggest IPO in American history. The company's valuation hits $70 billion at the end of the day's trading.

Judge Jackson rules that Microsoft broke American antitrust laws, using "technological shackles" to prevent rivals from competing with its Internet Explorer browser. Microsoft shares plummet in value, causing a new wave of volatility in the valuation of high-tech stocks. Cisco's market capitalisation creeps ahead of Microsoft's, making it the world's most valuable company.

Metallica, a rock band, forces the Napster music distribution network to remove 300,000 users, which it says pirated its music using the MP3 format. An American federal judge rules that MP3.com broke copyright law by collating 45,000 commercial CDs into its database, prompting the site to shut down its popular MyMP3 web-based distribution service.

Despite the warnings following 1999's

Melissa virus, the I Love You virus causes havoc on computers around the world, flooding e-mail networks and deleting users' music and graphics files. Microsoft is widely criticised for security holes in its Outlook e-mail program, said to be responsible for allowing the virus to propagate and destroy information.

As interest in wireless communications technology grows, the British government auctions off third-generation wide-spectrum bandwidth licences to mobile operators, raising £22.5 billion in the process. Germany announces plans to follow suit.

Boo.com, one of Europe's highest-profile online retailers, goes into liquidation after its widely criticised marketing strategy and complex design fail to create a profitable market for its sportswear and fashion goods. Valuations of European e-commerce companies fall rapidly as confidence among high-tech investors evaporates.

The total number of web pages reaches 1 billion.

2 Abbreviations

ADSL	Asynchronous Digital Subscriber Line
AOL	America Online
ASP	Active Server Pages
ATM	Asynchronous Transfer Mode or Adobe Type Manager
BBS	Bulletin Board System
BCC	Blind Carbon Copy
BPS	Bits Per Second
BRI	Basic Rate Interface
CAD	Computer Aided Design
CC	Carbon Copy
CCS	Cascading Style Sheet
CDA	Communications Decency Act
CDF	Channel Definition Format
CDMA	Code Division Multiple Access
CGI	Common Gateway Interface
COM	Component Object Model
CORBA	Common Object Request Broker Architecture
DCOM	Distributed Component Object Model
DES	Data Encryption Standard
DHCP	Dynamic Host Configuration Protocol
DHML	Dynamic Hypertext Mark-up Language
DOM	Document Object Model
DNS	Domain Name System
DSL	Digital Subscriber Line (or Loop)
EDI	Electronic Data Interchange
EFF	Electronic Frontier Foundation
FAQ	Frequently Asked Questions
FDM	Frequency-Division Multiplexing
FSF	Free Software Foundation
FTP	File Transfer Protocol
GIF	Graphics Interchange Format
GPRS	General Packet Radio Service
GSM	Global System for Mobile Communications
GUI	Graphical User Interface
HDML	Handheld Devices Mark-up Language
HTCPCP	Hyper Text Coffee Pot Control Protocol
HTML	Hypertext Mark-up Language
HTTP	Hypertext Transfer Protocol
IAB	Internet Architecture Board
IANA	Internet Assigned Names Authority
ICANN	Internet Corporation for Assigned

	Names and Numbers
ICQ	I Seek You
IETF	Internet Engineering Task Force
IMAP	Internet Message Access Protocol
IOTP	Internet Open Trading Protocol
IP	Internet Protocol
IPO	Initial Public Offering
IRC	Internet Relay Chat
IRL	In Real Life
ISDN	Integrated Services Digital Network
ISP	Internet Service Provider
JANET	Joint Academic Network
JIT	Just In Time
JPEG	Joint Picture Experts Group (or JPG)
Kbps	Kilobits per second
LAN	Local Area Network
LDAP	Lightweight Directory Access Protocol
LINX	London Internet Exchange
MAE	Metropolitan Area Exchange
MANAP	Manchester Network Access Point
Mbps	Millions of bits per second
Mbone	Multicast Backbone
MIME	Multipurpose Internet Mail Extensions
MOO	MUD Object Oriented
MSN	Microsoft Network
MPEG	Motion Picture Experts Group
MUD	Multi-user Dungeon
NAP	Network Access Point
NASDAQ	National Association of Securities Dealers Automated Quotation system
NC	Network Computer
NCSA	National Centre For Supercomputing Applications
NNTP	Network News Transport Protocol
OPS	Open Profiling Standard
ORB	Object Request Broker
OS	Operating System
OSI	Open Source Initiative
OSP	Online Service Provider
PANS	Public Access Network Services
PCS	Personal Communications Service
PDA	Personal Digital Assistant
PDF	Portable Document Format
PGP	Pretty Good Privacy

PKI	Public Key Infrastructure
PICS	Platform for Internet Content Selection
POP	Point of Presence
POP3	Post Office Protocol (latest version)
POTS	Plain Old Telephone Service
PPP	Point-to-Point Protocol
PPTP	Point-to-Point Tunnelling Protocol
PRI	Primary Rate Interface
PVC	Permanent Virtual Circuit
QoS	Quality of Service
RFC	Request For Comments
RSAC	Recreational Software Advisory Council
RSVP	ReSerVation Protocol
SDMI	Secure Digital Music Initiative
SET	Secure Electronic Transactions
SLIP	Serial Line Interface Protocol
SMTP	Simple Mail Transport Protocol
SQL	Structured Query Language
SSL	Secure Sockets Layer
TA	Terminal Adapter
TCP	Transmission Control Protocol
TCP/IP	Transmission Control Protocol/Internet Protocol
TDM	Time-Division Multiplexing
TLA	Three-Letter Acronym
TLD	Top-Level Domain
TTP	Trusted Third Party
URI	Uniform Resource Identifier
URL	Uniform Resource Locator
UUCP	Unix-to-Unix Copy Protocol
vBNS	Very High Speed Backbone Network Service
VM	Virtual Machine
VOIP	Voice Over IP
VPN	Virtual Private Network
VRML	Virtual Reality Modelling Language
W3C	World Wide Web Consortium
WAP	Wireless Application Protocol
WDM	Wavelength-Division Multiplexing
WELL	Whole Earth 'Lectronic Link
WIPO	World Intellectual Property Organisation
WML	Wireless Mark-up Language
XHTML	Extensible Hypertext Mark-up Language
XML	Extensible Mark-up Language
XSL	Extensible Stylesheet Language
XTLA	Extended Three-Letter Acronym

3 Internet tips

USING SEARCH ENGINES
- Don't rely on any one search engine or directory; they all have their strengths and weaknesses. Some are faster and some are more comprehensive in their coverage than others.
- Use a search engine appropriate for your information. In many cases, the local version of an engine or directory, such as yahoo.co.uk in the UK or lycos.fr in France, may yield better or more relevant results than their American parents.
- If individual search engines are not coming up with the goods try meta-engines such as webcrawler.com or askjeeves.com, which trawl a number of different information sources. Also look at software such as Copernic, which consults many search engines but also hunts directly through category-specific sites for information on a wide range of topics.
- Be as specific as you can. Searching for "Lamborghini" will yield better results than general concepts such as "Italian cars", or "sports cars".
- Investigate the advanced searching features of the main engines. All of them let you filter the information they return in some way; for example, by using a NOT or – operator to rule out areas that are of no interest. "Greenwich NOT Village" thus returns information on London's Thames-side location, excluding most of the references to New York. Likewise, the AND or + operator can be used to force the inclusion of particular terms in a search.
- Complete phrases return better results than isolated words. A phrase in quotation marks, such as "millennium dome", is much more likely to find the Greenwich construction than the two words alone.
- Ensure that sources are reliable. The web's

ability to operate as a vast game of Chinese whispers often corrupts so-called facts, so always try to check information back to its source. Most reliable sources of business information also include contact information; this may be the Internet age, but there is nothing wrong with using the phone to check facts.

CHOOSING AN ISP

- Pick a company with a reasonably long track record and a reputable name. BT, AOL and MSN are unlikely to go out of business in the near future, but the prospects of many newer ISPs, especially the free ones, are far from guaranteed.
- Check the pricing structure. Most ISPs now provide unlimited access for a basic monthly charge, but some still impose hourly charges. Some companies offer reduced rates for people who do not spend much time online, charging high excess fees if you exceed your allotted time.
- If you're a heavy Internet user, investigate an ISP's ISDN and ADSL offerings. Although these are considerably more expensive than dial-up connections, you get much faster access and, in the case of ADSL, an always-on connection, negating the need for dialling into your service provider every time you need access.
- In many areas, cable companies offer fast Internet access at rates that are competitive with the high-speed services from conventional ISPs. Like ADSL, cable connections are always on and provide high-speed access to the Internet, although they may suffer from overloading in busy areas.
- Many computer and Internet magazines publish ISP performance surveys on a regular basis, highlighting the fastest, most reliable and most consistent performers. Get some back issues and track the progress of prospective candidates over time.
- Make sure that a prospective ISP is up to date

with its software and standards. You should be provided with not just a browser but also an e-mail and newsreading package and FTP software. You should also check that the latest modem standards are supported. There are two distinct flavours of 56K modem, for example, so make sure they know about yours. If you use Macintosh computers, make certain that the ISP provides Mac versions of everything.

- If you work away from the office or home you may need e-mail forwarded to another account; a web-based e-mail service, for example. Check that your ISP provides this service. Also check its spam-filtering policy. Many ISPs are the targets of large-scale junk e-mailers, which is annoying at best and offensive at worst. Good ISPs should make a big effort to get rid of them.

- It's worth calling to check on an ISP's ability to handle large volumes of traffic. Good ISPs have a subscriber-to-modem ratio of less than 15:1 making it less likely that you'll get engaged tones when you dial in. It's also worth considering their ability to handle a sudden influx of new users (following a marketing drive, perhaps). Can they turn on extra bandwidth if needed? Ask if access is guaranteed. If you're turning over any part of your business to an ISP, you need to be sure of their level of commitment.

- Investigate support policies closely. If you need access to a helping hand around the clock, you'll need to make sure that an ISP offers 24-hour technical support services. Check also on the cost of these services. Some companies, notably the free ISPs, charge out support calls at premium rates.

- If you're planning to build your own website you'll need to host it somewhere. Many ISPs now provide web space on their servers for just this reason, but you may need to extend this service by increasing your disk space or using your own domain name, for example.

Check that your chosen ISP offers domain-hosting services, and make sure their costs are competitive. Also ask about the data kept about site visitors, and how often details of the log files will be sent to you. This is an important element in analysing the site's effectiveness.

PLANNING A WEB PRESENCE

- Modern software packages make the DIY approach to websites practical. These can create everything from simple one-page sites to complete transactional e-commerce ventures, although the latter is not trivial for those with limited experience of development projects.
- Creating a site in-house ensures maximum control, but even basic sites impose substantial time costs. web development always takes longer than expected, and updating content is a job that should not be underestimated.
- Remember that in many markets there is nothing wrong with the oft-maligned brochureware idea. Simple sites can do an excellent job of attracting new overseas customers, for example, or simply educating existing or local ones. Think hard about what you're trying to achieve before embarking on any development project, and don't hang on the bells and whistles until you're sure they add something useful to the site.
- The success of your site depends on people visiting it, so research online marketing techniques carefully. Find out how to register the site with all the important search engines and directories. It's worth looking at services such as Submit-it, which for a fee will handle this job for you. Similarly, look at the LinkExchange system to get some ideas on advertising your site elsewhere on the web.
- If you decide to use an outside agency to build your website, apply all the same rules that you would when sourcing any other

expensive item. Check their previous experience, look at examples of sites they've built and, most critically, check their ability to understand your business. What other resources can they access? Don't get carried away in the hype.

- Think ahead as far as you can, and plan for growth of the site. Can the site you need today be easily expanded to encompass future needs, such as capturing information about users or conducting electronic credit card transactions? Will your ISP cope with or tolerate thousands of visitors without imposing excess bandwidth charges?

- Is the site secure? Can outsiders get at sensitive e-mail or details of customers and transactions? Is the computer on which the site lives safe from fire or water damage, theft or vandalism? Is the code and content backed up somewhere safe? If in doubt, ask your ISP or developer. Mistakes can be extremely costly.

- Look carefully at the opportunities offered by the new small business portals, such as Microsoft's bCentral in the United States or Virgin's BizNet in the UK. Most of these services can help design and build sites, register them automatically with the important search engines and generally provide lots of assistance in building and managing an effective web presence.

CONNECTING ON THE MOVE

- First, decide whether you need the capabilities of a full-blown PC or Macintosh while connecting on the move. If you need to visit complex websites in all their glory, or transfer and edit large files created in applications such as word processors or spreadsheets, you'll almost certainly need a laptop computer. If all you need is e-mail and some basic text-only web access, a much smaller and more portable PDA will do, such as a 3Com Palm device or a Psion.

- Consider how flexible you need to be when

connecting. If you're likely to be in an office or other building, you'll probably need a standard modem that connects to a wall socket. If you need to check mail at all times – on trains or buses, for example – you'll need a slower (and, usually, more expensive) wireless connection via a mobile phone.

- If you decide on a wireless connection, consider finding an ISP that provides specific support for your phone provider. Mobile-to-mobile connections are generally faster and more stable than mobile-to-landline calls, resulting in faster data transfer and fewer dropped calls.

- When travelling abroad, check whether your ISP maintains overseas POPs (points of presence), thus enabling you to dial in on a local number. The large ISPs such as AOL, Compuserve and MSN all have operations worldwide, and many smaller companies now provide other ways for subscribers to connect by making local calls.

- Before setting off on your travels, make sure that software on laptops is set up properly. Operating systems such as Windows 95 allow you to specify your dialling location, setting up the relevant options accordingly; for example, your home settings would not include dialling 9 for an outside line.

- If you have a POP3 e-mail account, remember that you can check it from the most popular web-based e-mail services such as Hotmail. This makes it easy to collect your mail from any machine with a browser, without the need to know local access numbers or dialling in long-distance.

- When considering palmtop devices for connecting to the Internet on the move, make sure that they are equipped with synchronisation software for keeping your PC and your handheld in tune with one another. You can then compose and reply to e-mails on the road and transfer them to a desktop machine when you get home or to the office.

Most palmtop and handheld devices now interface neatly with programs such as Microsoft Outlook.

- If you're using a standard modem cable, always take a range of phone socket adapters with you when you travel alongside the necessary power adapters. It may not be possible to get the right converters in the country you're visiting, making it impossible to connect your computer to the local telephone system.

- Remember that in some cases you may not actually need an e-mail program to communicate electronically. If you own a mobile phone, investigate the possibilities of SMS messaging. Although SMS messages are short (160 characters), they can nonetheless be useful for sending quick messages to other SMS subscribers. You could also investigate companies that provide e-mail-to-SMS gateways, such as Airmail in the UK. These essentially provide an e-mail address for your phone. E-mail sent to that address appears as one or more SMS messages. When you reply the conversion happens the other way.

- Don't forget about Internet cafés. Even the most experienced Internet users have disasters sometimes, and the local café is often a lifesaver. Most cities around the world have more than enough for your needs.

DOWNLOADING SOFTWARE

- Make a point of checking the software sections of sites such as www.microsoft.com and home.netscape.com for updates and bug fixes for your browser software. It is especially important to keep an eye on security updates. Some new viruses, for example, can be screened out by updating files in your browser and/or mail client. Also look out for extra programs from your software makers, which add to or improve on the originals in some way.

- Always look for the fastest available

connection from which to download your software. Many download sites are extremely busy, especially local sites at peak times of the day, so it's worth hunting around for a quieter site. Most download sites will give you a choice of locations (called mirror sites) from which to download a particular program. Choose one in a part of the world that is likely to be quiet at that time of the day.

- You don't always have to download a file from its home page. Instead, use the file-finding feature of search engines to locate a less busy place to get it from. It's easy to find out the name of the file you want, even from the busiest sites. Once you have it, use the FTP Search facility at Lycos, for example, to locate a place nearer home that has the file you're looking for.

- You shouldn't need to download important software very often. Once you have your collection of essential browsers, e-mail clients and other software tools, keep copies of the set-up files you downloaded somewhere safe; preferably on a high-capacity disk such as a Zip disk rather than a floppy.

- Remember that many useful software tools are either completely free or can be tried out before you buy them. Examples of the sorts of things that often come in useful are file decompression utilities, graphics software and network optimisation programs. There are many examples of these, located at many thousands of sites scattered around the Internet (see Recommended sites).

- Always screen downloaded programs for viruses, even if you think they come from a reliable source. It's wise to invest in a reliable virus checker that automatically checks not just software but also Microsoft Office documents, Outlook e-mail and invisible programs running on web pages. All of these can conceal hostile and potentially dangerous code.

SHOPPING

- Shopping online with a credit card is very safe – in most cases, safer than in the real world. Even so, it is a good idea to limit its exposure. Look for retail sites that keep your card details on a secure server, so you don't have to resend it every time you buy something. If you're worried about the vulnerability of the server or the company's policy about use of the credit card, call and ask for details of their security system. Many companies will happily accept credit card details by fax rather than e-mail or direct connection.
- Make sure that your browser is set up for secure connections to the Internet. If it is, a small padlock will appear in the program's status bar when you connect to a secure server, indicating that the data being passed between your computer and the remote one is safe from prying eyes. If you're in any doubt about this, consult the relevant pages on the browser manufacturer's website or look at the help system.
- Shop around for the best deals. Many things are much cheaper to buy from Internet sites than from stores, and online retailers are competing vigorously to bring prices down still further. In many countries, the seven things most commonly bought on the Internet – books, software, music, travel, computer hardware, clothing and electronics – each have several sites devoted to them, with many special deals being offered on a weekly or even daily basis.
- Investigate aggregate buying sites such as Mercata.com in America or Letsbuyit.com in Europe. These operate on the basis that the more people who want something, the cheaper that thing becomes. Although the range of goods on offer is still fairly restricted, it is likely to grow as more people are attracted to this form of shopping.
- Auctions can be a fun way of buying things online, but don't get carried away with the

novelty of it. It is easy to end up paying considerably more for your goods than you would locally.

- Watch out for advertising in the mainstream media. Many people selling goods on the Internet are targeting consumers with television and cinema campaigns rather than online marketing.
- Consider buying goods from overseas. A retailer in a different country is no less inherently safe than one in your own street, and is often a good deal cheaper. American CDs, for example, cost about half as much as identical discs bought in the UK. When buying from overseas retailers always check delivery costs. Most international retailers offer a range of delivery options from standard airmail to fast courier services.
- Look for special features that make it easier for you to shop. Amazon's 1-Click ordering is a good example; since it already has your details, it can process a buying request with a single click rather than a lengthy checkout process. Another example is some fashion retailers, which allow you to view their clothes from several angles to give you a clearer idea of how they look when worn.
- Keep an eye on specialist sites like lastminute.com, which sell not only cheap flights and holidays but other occasional items too, such as cars and mobile phones. Remember also that all sorts of new ways of doing old things are being hatched on such sites. Budget, a car hire firm, lets you specify how much you're prepared to pay for your hire car, rather than giving you a fixed price.
- Remember that you can buy a huge range of things on the Internet. Although most of the volume is in books, CDs, software and hardware, sites are popping up all over the place selling things you might find it hard to get anywhere else. (Queensland mud crabs, anyone?) Spend some time looking for interesting sites using the main search engines.

4 Recommended websites

Here are some websites recommended by people who work for or read *The Economist*. The lists are inevitably somewhat eclectic and do not pretend to include all the websites that are worth recommending. As far as possible, every effort has been made to check that the addresses given are accurate. If you have any comments or suggestions that we might take into account for future editions, please send them to the publishers at info@profilebooks.co.uk

BOOKS (SECOND-HAND, OTHER)
www.bibliofind.com
A searchable collection of used and rare books, periodicals and ephemera for sale
www.bibliomania.com
Collection of classic novels, poetry, drama, dictionaries and non-fiction works
www.concordance.com
Allows word searches through 600 classics
www.gh.cs.su.oz.au/~matty/Shakespeare
The Bard's plays and poems in full
www.promo.net/pg
Official site of Project Gutenberg, aimed at making information, books and other materials available free to the public electronically

BOOKSHOPS (NEW)
www.amazon.com
The web's most famous bookshop
www.amazon.co.uk
British subsidiary of Amazon.com
www.bn.com
Giant US bookshop
www.bol.com
German media giant Bertelsmann's bookshop, catering for the European market
www.books.co.uk
Directory and descriptions of the UK's online booksellers
www.bookshop.co.uk
British bookshop

www.fatbrain.com
Specialises in professional books and interactive training and certification courses

BUSINESS
adage.com
The *Advertising Age*, a worldwide marketing and advertising industry newspaper
cbs.marketwatch.com
Rich source of market and economic news for investors from the CBS stable
mckinseyquarterly.com/home.htm
Library of articles and research from the management consultancy McKinsey
strategis.ic.gc.ca
Canadian business information site, featuring company directories, trade and investment resources and economic analysis
www.acca-usa.org
Association of Chartered Certified Accountants site, listing many accounting resources
www.accountingweb.co.uk
British accountants' community
www.bnet.co.uk
A source of practical management information for British businesses
www.carol.co.uk
Company annual reports and other investor information
www.ceoexpress.com
Huge list of well-organised links to key business, Internet, media, finance and many other resources
www.e-business.pwcglobal.com
PricewaterhouseCoopers' e-business site
www.eiu.com
Global business information and analysis from the Economist Intelligence Unit, part of The Economist Group
www.euro-emu.co.uk
Emunet, a resource devoted to Europe's single currency
www.ft.com
The *Financial Times*, an excellent source for

international business news

`www.gbn.org`
Home of the Global Business Network, with a forum for members' exchanges

`www.globalsources.com`
Product and trade information and links for volume buyers of consumer, business and industrial goods

`www.guru.com`
Network for professionals and independent contractors

`www.hoovers.com`
Global company directory with financial data, company news and links

`www.iisg.nl/~w3vl`
The World Wide Web Virtual Library's guide to the history of labour and business

`www.oanda.com`
Olsen and Associates' currency resource, including forecasts, historical tables and converters

`www.propertymall.co.uk`
News and property information for the commercial-property industry in Britain

`www.smartmoney.com`
The *Wall Street Journal*'s magazine of personal business, including a customisable portfolio tracker

`www.strategy-business.com`
Community site for business leaders encouraging the exchange of new business ideas, including articles and book reviews

`www.thebiz.co.uk`
Business directory and database with a strong British focus

`www.thomasregister.com`
Searchable database of brand names, products and services from the Thomas Register of American manufacturers

`www.ukindustry.co.uk/ukidir.htm`
A directory of British companies categorised by industry

`www.virginbiz.net`
Portal for small businesses, with strategies for starting a dot.com company

www.wsj.com
The *Wall Street Journal*'s Europe, US and Asia
editions available on a subscription basis

CENTRAL BANKS
www.bankofengland.co.uk
The Bank of England
www.bis.org
The Bank for International Settlements, the
central bank of central banks
www.bis.org./cbanks.htm
Links to central banks around the world
www.bog.frb.fed.us
US Federal Reserve
www.boj.or.jp/en
The Bank of Japan
www.bundesbank.de
The Bundesbank
www.ecb.int
The European Central Bank
www.patriot.net/users/bernkopf
A central-banking resource centre, with good
links to international central banks

CURRENT AFFAIRS: AFRICA
polyglot.lss.wisc.edu/afrst/links.html
The University of Wisconsin's catalogue of Africa
links
www.afbis.com/analysis/index.htm
Articles on business and investment from the UK-
based charity Africa Economic Analysis
www.africanews.org/index.html
Africa News Online, with wide geographical and
topical coverage
www.mbendi.co.za
Pan-African business encyclopaedia
www.mg.co.za
Daily Mail and *Guardian* newspaper website,
covering news from all African countries
www.north-africa.com
Website of the *North Africa Journal*, a weekly
monitor of current affairs in Algeria, Morocco,
Tunisia and other North African countries

CURRENT AFFAIRS: ASIA

www.asiamedia.ucla.edu
News, views and links from the Asia Pacific
Media Network
www.CNN.com/AsiaNow
CNN's Asian news and analysis

CURRENT AFFAIRS: EAST ASIA

business-times.asia1.com.sg
The *Business Times* of Singapore, a leading
business daily with coverage throughout South-
East Asia
coombs.anu.edu.au/WWWVL-
AsianStudies.html
World Wide Web Virtual Library site on Asian
studies, with coverage of China, Hong Kong,
Taiwan, Singapore and other Asian countries
members.tripod.com/mbionat
Compilation of Western news articles on the
Philippines
straitstimes.asia1.com.sg
The *Straits Times*, based in Singapore but with
coverage throughout Asia
www.bangkokpost.co.th
The *Bangkok Post*
www.fmprc.gov.cn/english/dhtml
China's Ministry of Foreign Affairs
www.insidechina.com
News on China from the European Internet
Network
www.japanecho.co.jp
A bi-monthly journal featuring English
translations of essays, interviews and discussions
on Japanese politics and economics
www.japantimes.co.jp
The *Japan Times*
www.mofa.go.jp
Japan's Ministry of Foreign Affairs
www.mofa.gov.tw/emofa/eindex.htm
Taiwan's Ministry of Foreign Affairs
www.nni.nikkei.co.jp
The Nikkei Net Interactive, jam-packed with 24-
hour business news from Japan available on a
paying subscription (with free trial) basis

`www.scmp.com`
The daily *South China Morning Post*, including extensive news coverage of Hong Kong, China and Asia
`www.taiwansecurity.org`
Taiwanese news and current affairs

CURRENT AFFAIRS: SOUTH ASIA

`indiaworld.com`
Indian national and political news and current affairs
`www.cmie.com`
The Centre for Monitoring Indian Economy
`www.dawn.com`
Pakistan's English-language paper
`www.economictimes.com`
India's *Economic Times*, covering companies, industry, economics and politics
`www.timesofindia.com`
The *Times of India*
`www.pak-economist.com`
The *Pakistan Economist*, a Pakistani business magazine

CURRENT AFFAIRS: US AND CANADA

`www.abcnews.com`
ABC News
`www.cnn.com`
CNN
`www.drudgereport.com`
Famous and sometimes newsbreaking site, with links to many others
`www.epn.org`
Economics and social policy recommendations from the Electronic Policy Network, allied with the *American Prospect* and the Economic Policy Institute
`www.globeandmail.ca`
The *Globe and Mail*, Canada's national newspaper
`www.house.gov`
The official site of the US House of Representatives
`www.ipl.org/ref/POTUS`
Presidents of the United States site, containing

background information on every president to date, election results, cabinet members, and notable events
www.latimes.com
The *Los Angeles Times*
www.motherjones.com
Daily news for sceptical citizens
www.nationalpost.com
Canadian newspaper
www.nytimes.com
The *New York Times*
www.policy.com
A vast public policy resource, with news and in-depth analysis
www.public-policy.org
Public policy site with links to US and Canadian members' websites
www.rollcall.com
Roll Call, the Capitol Hill watchdog of The Economist Group
www.senate.gov
The official site for the US Senate
www.slate.com
Microsoft's *Slate* magazine, containing analysis of national media coverage and its own acerbic views of the world
www.usatoday.com
USA Today
www.washingtonpost.com
The *Washington Post*
www.whitehouse.gov
The US White House official site

CURRENT AFFAIRS: UK

www.fco.gov.uk
The UK's Foreign & Commonwealth Office
www.guardian.co.uk
Guardian Unlimited, the web version of the *Guardian*, a left-leaning daily
www.independent.co.uk
The *Independent*, a centre-left news daily
www.open.gov.uk
Links to public-sector organisations in the UK

www.parliament.uk
The British Parliament's website, including
sections for the House of Lords and the House of
Commons and the text of Parliament's daily
journal *Hansard*
www.ukpol.co.uk
Political resource with links to thousands of
political sites
www.telegraph.co.uk
The Electronic Telegraph, the online version of
the conservative *Daily Telegraph*
www.the-times.co.uk
The *Times*, a British daily in the political centre

CURRENT AFFAIRS: EUROPE

europa.eu.int
The European Union's official site, including
statistics and links to the Parliament, Court of
Justice and other EU sites
www.austria.org
Austrian press and information service from
Washington, DC
www.bcemag.com
Articles from *Business Central Europe*, published
by The Economist Group
www.ce-review.org
Central European affairs, as covered by the
Central and East European New Media Initiative
(CEENMI)
www.ecmi.de
European Centre for Minority Issues, which
promotes interdisciplinary research on minority-
majority relations in Europe
www.einmedia.com
European Internet Network hub site, with links
to Central Europe Online, Czech Today, Hungary
Today, Poland Today, Romania Today, Slovakia
Today, Slovenia Today and Yugoslavia Today
www.european-voice.com
A weekly newspaper on EU affairs, published by
The Economist Group
www.euroscanner.com
Well-organised search engine for finding sites
relevant to the single currency

`www.handelsblatt.de/englishsum`
English-language summaries available from
Handelsblatt, Germany's business and financial
daily

`www.moscowtimes.ru`
The *Moscow Times*

`www.nato.int`
The North Atlantic Treaty Organisation's website,
complete with news and an archive of all official
NATO documents

`www.praguereport.com`
Daily English-language news from the Czech
Republic, with links to similar Warsaw and
Budapest services

`www.rferl.org`
News coverage and analysis of Central and
Eastern Europe and the former Soviet Union
from Radio Free Europe/Radio Liberty

`www.russiajournal.com`
Russian business and news journal, with a special
focus on foreign trade, investment and markets

`www.swissinfo.org`
Swiss news and current affairs, from Swiss Radio
International

`www.times.spb.ru`
The *St Petersburg Times*, affiliated with the
Moscow Times

CURRENT AFFAIRS: MIDDLE EAST

`gulf2000.columbia.edu`
Trove of information on the eight countries of
the Persian Gulf region

`www.a7.org`
The independent Arutz Sheva Israeli national
radio station

`www.arabia.com`
Arabia Online, including current affairs, business
news and cultural coverage from the Arab world

`www.ariga.com`
Site dedicated to coverage of the various peace
movements in the Middle East

`www.fas.harvard.edu/~mideast/inMEres/`
`inMEres.html`
Harvard's vast library of links to Middle East

websites
www.haaretzdaily.com
English-language version of the *Haaretz* daily
www.jpost.com
Internet edition of the *Jerusalem Post*, Israel's
main English-language daily
www.mfa.gov.il
Israel's Ministry of Foreign Affairs site, providing
detailed information on the Israeli government
and its policies

CURRENT AFFAIRS: OCEANIA
theage.com.au
The *Age*, Melbourne's daily newspaper
www.abc.net.au
Australian Broadcasting Corporation
www.nzherald.co.nz
The *New Zealand Herald*, with news from
Auckland and the nation
www.smh.com.au
The *Sydney Morning Herald*

CURRENT AFFAIRS: SOUTH & CENTRAL AMERICA
lanic.utexas.edu
The Latin American Network Information Center,
providing a well-organised encyclopaedia of
links broken down by category and by country
lcweb2.loc.gov/hlas/hlashome.html
The *Handbook of Latin American Studies*, with a
searchable bibliography of scholarly works on
Latin America published by the Library of
Congress and links to the Library's Hispanic
Reading Room
lib.nmsu.edu/subject/bord/laguia
Directory of organisations, news sources and
scholarly resources addressing Latin American
issues
www.brazzil.com
Monthly Brazilian magazine focusing on current
affairs
www.cidac.org
Center for Research and Development, with
analysis of Mexico's politics and economy

www.latinfinance.com
A monthly magazine of investment news from Latin America
www.latinnews.com
General news from Latin America

CURRENT AFFAIRS: WORLD

lcweb2.loc.gov/frd/cs
Good but not always up-to-date country-by-country information from the Library of Congress
news.bbc.co.uk
BBC News
nobelprizes.com/nobel
Biographical information on Nobel Prize winners current and past, with good links
stratfor.com
International news and analysis
www.1stheadlines.com
News headlines from key global media, including business, sports and technology sections
www.agora.stm.it/elections/election.htm
Round-up of elections and electoral websites around the world
www.economist.com
Global news, opinion and analysis from *The Economist*
www.g7.utoronto.ca
G8 summit information centre
www.gksoft.com/govt/en
Centralised resource for linking to individual countries' government sites
www.icrc.org
The International Committee of the Red Cross
www.iea.org
International Energy Agency site, including statistics and world energy outlook
www.iht.com
The *International Herald Tribune*
www.imf.org
The International Monetary Fund
www.intl-crisis-group.org
The International Crisis Group, a think-tank with analysis and reports on conflicts in Algeria, Bosnia, Cambodia, Central Africa and the Balkans

www.un.org
The United Nations

ECONOMICS

ce.cei.gov.cn
Government website on the Chinese economy
csf.colorado.edu/pkt
Archive of post-Keynesian thought
epinet.org
Economic issues and trends discussed by the
Economic Policy Institute
utip.gov.utexas.edu
Inequality indicators and analysis from the
University of Texas
web.mit.edu/krugman/www
MIT professor Paul Krugman's view of the
economic world
www.bea.doc.gov
Economic data and analysis compiled by the
Bureau of Economic Analysis, part of the US
Department of Commerce
www.brook.edu
The Brookings Institution, a politically centre
Washington think-tank
www.businesscycle.com
Economic Cycle Research Institute site, discussing
causes and predictions of economic cycles
www.dismal.com
The *Dismal Scientist*, a review and analysis of
current economic news and trends
www.diw-berlin.de
The German Institute for Economic Research
www.fao.org
The UN's Food and Agriculture Organisation
website
www.fmcenter.org
Information, research and analysis of the Federal
Reserve and financial markets from the non-
profit Financial Markets Center
www.geocities.com/WallStreet/8691
Statistics and analysis of the Canadian economy
www.iie.com
The Institute for International Economics

www.ilo.org
The International Labour Organization
www.imf.org
The International Monetary Fund
www.internetindicators.com/index.html
Round-up of Internet economy indicators
www.levy.org
The Jerome Levy Institute, with papers on
economic policy analysis
www.marxists.org
The Marxists Internet Archive in 14 languages
www.nabe.com
The National Association for Business Economists
www.nber.org
The National Bureau of Economic Research
www.nic.in/stat
Indian economic statistics
www.oecd.org
The Organisation for Economic Co-operation and
Development
www.res.org.uk
The UK's Royal Economic Society
www.tutor2u.com
An economics tutor, complete with quizzes
www.vanderbilt.edu/AEA
The American Economic Association
www.worldbank.org
The World Bank
www.wto.org
The World Trade Organization
www1.ifs.org.uk
The UK's Institute for Fiscal Studies

EMPLOYMENT

careers.wsj.com
The *Wall Street Journal*'s careers section
jobasia.com
Large Asian recruitment website
www.adecco.com
Job-finding site from one of the world's largest
recruitment companies
www.adecco.co.uk
British branch of adecco.com

www.cityjobs.co.uk
Well-organised site for job postings in Britain
www.cofinders.com
Helps start-ups to find partners
www.emdsnet.com
Global recruitment services from EMDS, an
international consultancy
www.latpro.com
Latin American professional recruitment website,
for Spanish and Portuguese speakers
www.pianetalavoro.ch
Recruitment site for jobs in Switzerland and
northern Italy
www.referencenow.com
Meeting place for job applicants and employers
www.vaultreports.com
Careers information and employment research
site
www.workoplis.com
Canadian careers site
www.workunlimited.co.uk
Careers website from the *Guardian*, a British
newspaper

ENTERTAINMENT
dpsinfo.com
The Dead People Server, for finding out if celebs
are still alive
www.atomfilms.com
Short entertainment e-hub, with films lasting
from 30 seconds to 30 minutes
www.bored.com
"Links to the most interesting sites on the
Internet", according to its propaganda
www.boxofficeguru.com
Site focusing on the success or otherwise of the
latest Hollywood films
www.eonline.com
The standard-bearer for American entertainment
reporting
www.ifilm.com
Film portal with downloadable videos, reviews,
links, news and more

www.imdb.com
Large web database of film information
www.launch.com
Vast assemblage of music videos, audio, concert
listings and artist features across all music genres
www.moviecritic.com
Film-recommendation site based on personal
ratings
www.real.com
Streaming media from Real Networks, including
news, film clips, live music and live radio
www.shockrave.com
Downloadable games showing off the features of
Macromedia's Shockwave technology
www.thesmokinggun.com
Documentation of the bizarre: uncensored court
documents, FBI files and more on extraneous or
important subjects
www.timeout.com
Indispensable guide to London nightlife, with
guides to 32 other cities
www.variety.com
The scoop, and the numbers, on the
entertainment industry

FINANCE

www.bloomberg.com
Financial market updates and analysis from
Bloomberg
www.ebrd.com
The European Bank for Reconstruction and
Development, which invests in Eastern Europe
www.fiafii.org/default.asp
The Futures Industry Association
www.globalfindata.com
Current and historical financial data
www.hedgeindex.com
Statistical database on hedge fund performance
www.ifc.org
The International Finance Corporation
www.marhedge.com
News bulletins and information on hedge funds
www.napf.co.uk
The UK's National Association of Pension Funds,

representing the occupational pensions
movement
www.reuters.com
Financial updates from Reuters
www.sec.gov
The Securities and Exchange Commission
www.stockcharts.com
Free stock charting, market analysis and financial
tools
www.thestreet.com
Detailed reports and analysis from Wall Street

HEALTH
dir.yahoo.com/health
Yahoo's directory of health sites
jama.ama-assn.org
The *Journal of the American Medical Association*
www.bmj.com
The *British Medical Journal*
www.cdc.gov
The US Center for Disease Control, with
information for international travellers
www.healthfinder.org
Gateway to consumer health and human services
information, provided by the US Department of
Health and Human Services
www.healthgate.com
Health and lifestyle recommendations and news
www.nih.gov
The US National Institutes for Health
www.nlm.nih.gov
US National Library of Medicine site, with a link
to the Medline database of health information
www.omni.ac.uk
Organising Medical Networked Information, a
British gateway to biomedical Internet resources
www.who.org
The World Health Organisation

HUMOUR AND GAMES
www.cybercheeze.com
Huge joke archive, including a Joke of the Day
e-mail service

www.darwinawards.com
A celebration of Darwin, recognising those who improve the gene pool by removing themselves from it in interesting ways

www.dilbert.com
Scott Adams' course in people management skills, or lack thereof

www.doonesbury.com
The great political cartoonist

www.improb.com
A look at brand new ways to waste research funds, including the Ig Noble awards

www.station.sony.com
Sony's game site, featuring versions of Jeopardy, Wheel of Fortune and Trivial Pursuit

www.theonion.com
Satirical newspaper poking fun at politics, media and anything newsworthy

INTERNET

www.alertbox.com
Jakob Nielsen's respected bi-weekly analysis of website design and navigability

www.cnet.com/internet/0-3773.html
CNET's hub on browser technology, featuring comparative reviews, software updates, hints and tips, links and more

www.commerce.net
The e-commerce industry association's site, with a range of interesting resources, a research centre and the latest e-commerce news

www.download.com
Source of free and try-before-you-buy software on the web

www.eff.org
Organisation devoted to the protection of civil liberties on the Internet, especially privacy and free speech

www.icra.org
Organisation helping parents and others to filter Internet content

www.ietf.org
The Internet Engineering Task Force

www.internet.com
Massive site providing well-organised links to thousands of other resources

www.isoc.org
The Internet Society, which works to develop Internet standards and education. Source of news, discussion groups and conference information

www.java.sun.com
Cradle of Sun's ground-breaking web technology, and the web's most comprehensive Java resource

www.linux.org
Home to Linux, a rare Windows competitor, with links, software, events, explanations, shopping and more

www.opensource.org
Site offering different views of the open-source software movement, with links to relevant resources

www.sdmi.org
An initiative devoted to the protection of digital musical copyright, whose members include most of the big players in music and technology around the world

www.searchenginewatch.com
Loads of information on search engines, including performance comparisons and tips for users

www.w3c.org
The guiding light for the World Wide Web, and the source of a vast quantity of technical specifications and historical information

JOURNAL DIRECTORIES
www.helsinki.fi/WebEc/journals.html
Huge list of links to economics journals on the web

www.mediafinder.com
Covers over 90,000 publications

www.publist.com
Large directory of journals and periodicals

LAW
www.abanet.org
The American Bar Association

www.abanet.org/ceeli
The American Bar Association's Central and East
European Law Initiative
www.americanlawyer.com
The *American Lawyer*, the leading US monthly
on law
www.asil.org
American Society of International Law
www.clubi.ie/competition
Site for *Competition*, a journal specialising in EU
antitrust law and the regulation of utilities, with
antitrust law links
www.european-patent-office.org
The European Patent Office
www.hg.org
Law and government portal
www.law.com
Legal information
www.lawsoc.org.uk
The Law Society of England and Wales
www.uspto.gov
The US Patent and Trade Office

PERSONAL FINANCE

finance.yahoo.com
Yahoo's extensive financial resources for
individuals and small businesses
moneycentral.msn.com/home.asp
Personal finance resource for American users,
with sections on saving and spending,
retirement, wills, tax and much more
www.fool.com
Home of the Motley Fool, one of the web's best-
established sources of financial advice, with a
site specific to Britain too
www.ftyourmoney.com
High-quality information from the *Financial
Times*, covering saving, investing, mortgages, tax,
insurance and more
www.moneyworld.co.uk
Advice for savers and investors in Britain
www.oft.gov.uk/html/finance
Finance advice from the UK's Office of Fair
Trading

www.quicken.com
Personal finance news and tools from Intuit
www.verticalone.com
One-stop shopping for tracking personal finance
www.yodlee.com
Similar services to VerticalOne, above
www.zdii.com/fp.asp
Interactive investor site

REFERENCE

gwis2.circ.gwu.edu/~gprice/listof.htm
A central clearing house and search engine for
the vast number of lists of information on the
Internet
www.about.com
Expert guides on thousands of subjects, each
with dozens of links and other web resources
www.britannica.com
More than just the *Encyclopedia Britannica*
www.encyclopedia.com
14,000 well-organised free entries from the
Concise Columbia Electronic Encyclopedia
www.framed.usps.com/ncsc/lookups/
lookup_zip+4.html
Zip-code directory from the US Postal Service
www.gurunet.com
Useful dictionary tool for checking words on
web pages or other documents
www.mapquest.com
Extensive global mapping and travel service
www.odci.gov/cia/publications/factbook
The *CIA World Factbook*, with vital statistics and
information on every country
www.phonenet.bt.com:8080
BT's telephone directory
www.royalmail.co.uk/paf/home.htm
The Royal Mail's postcode finder
www.streetmap.co.uk
Site displaying Britain's street maps by area or
postcode, including street maps of Greater
London and road atlas maps of mainland Britain
www.xe.net/ucc/full.shtml
Universal currency converter

SCIENCE

`scicentral.com`
Reports and daily news from all areas of
scientific research
`unisci.com`
Regular round-up of science news from
American universities
`www.astronomynow.com`
Popular British astronomy magazine
`www.chemsoc.org`
The Chemistry Society
`www.cid.harvard.edu/cidbiotech/links.`
`htm`
Biotechnology links from Harvard's Center for
International Development
`www.esa.int`
European Space Agency site, with regular
updates on European developments
`www.howthingswork.com`
How Stuff Works, a self-explanatory site covering
everything from computers to caffeine
`www.inconstantmoon.com`
Daily updates of images of the Moon
`www.mars2030.net`
The Mars Millennium project, challenging
students to design a Mars-based community
`www.nasa.gov`
Home to NASA, the US space program
`www.newscientist.com`
Populist science news from the *New Scientist*
`www.newshub.com/science`
Science headlines from the world's premier news
sources
`www.nytimes.com/yr/mo/day/national/`
`index-science.html`
Daily science and health coverage from the *New
York Times*
`www.sciam.com`
Scientific American
`www.sciencedaily.com/index.htm`
Daily news site specialising in research
`www.sciencenews.org`
Weekly science news magazine

`www.usno.navy.mil`
The US Naval Observatory's website, detailing activities from measuring the positions and motions of celestial objects to measuring the Earth's rotation

SEARCH ENGINES

`search.netscape.com`
Netscape
`www.alltheweb.com`
Fast search
`www.altavista.com`
AltaVista
`www.askjeeves.com`
Question and answer service
`www.deja.com`
DejaNews (newsgroup search engine)
`www.excite.com`
Excite
`www.google.com`
Google
`www.lycos.com`
Lycos
`www.northernlight.com`
Northern Light
`www.yahoo.com`
Yahoo

SHOPPING

`www.ebay.com`
Auction-format trading site for an endless variety of items
`www.etoys.com`
Online toyshop, with a British subsidiary
`www.intersaver.co.uk`
Low-cost electronic household goods from most major manufacturers
`www.lastminute.com`
British site for last-minute bookings – travel, entertainment, restaurants and gifts
`www.letsbuyit.com`
European collective buying site: the more buyers there are for an item, the cheaper it gets

www.maplink.com
Huge inventory of maps for sale
www.mercata.com
American collective buying site
www.shopping.com
Huge shopping portal from the AltaVista stable,
with reviews, ratings and hints for shopping online
www.shopsmart.com
UK-based shopping gateway to over 900
retailers, and a PriceScan feature for finding the
lowest prices
www.virgin.net
Entertainment and leisure site with a huge list of
British retailers and their websites
www.walmart.com
American retail giant

SPORT

cbs.sportsline.com
Mammoth site devoted principally to US sports
espn.go.com
The American sporting monolith's vast website,
for followers of US sports
news.bbc.co.uk/hi/english/sport/
default.stm
World sports coverage from the BBC
rivals.com
American site focusing on team loyalties rather
than blanket coverage, with chat rooms and
other facilities for fans
www.cricket.org
Cricket site with ball-by-ball coverage of
international games, extensive player information
and many interviews and articles
www.ft.com/sport
The business of sport, from the *Financial Times*
www.sportal.com
Major sports hub, with an emphasis on European
football
www.sportlive.net
Sports site focused on Britain with competitions,
interactive games and daily sports diaries by e-mail
www.uefa.com
Union of European Football Associations

STATISTICS

`europa.eu.int/en/comm/eurostat/`
`serven/part8/8d.htm`
The European Union's list of statistics agencies worldwide

`petra.istat.it`
Italy's National Statistical Institute

`stats.bls.gov/oreother.htm`
The US Bureau of Labor Statistics, with links to other statistics agencies worldwide

`www.abs.gov.au`
The Australian Bureau of Statistics

`www.cbs.gov.il/engindex.htm`
Israel's Central Bureau of Statistics

`www.cbs.nl/en/index.htm`
Dutch social statistics and economic indicators

`www.cso.ie`
Ireland's Central Statistics Office

`www.dst.dk`
Denmark's statistical site

`www.fedstats.gov`
One-stop shop for US federal statistics, from over 70 US agencies

`www.ine.es`
Spain's National Statistical Institute

`www.ine.pt`
Portugal's statistics institute

`www.insee.fr/va/index.htm`
France's National Institute of Statistics and Economic Studies

`www.ons.gov.uk`
The UK's Office for National Statistics

`www.singstat.gov.sg`
Statistics Singapore

`www.ssb.no/english`
Norwegian central store for national statistics and economic indicators

`www.stat.go.jp`
Japan's Statistics Bureau & Statistics Centre

`www.statbel.fgov.be/home_en.htm`
Belgium's National Institute of Statistics

`www.statice.is`
Statistics Iceland

www.statistik.admin.ch/eindex.htm
Swiss Federal Statistical Office
www.statistik-bund.de
Germany's Federal Statistical Office
www.statssa.gov.za
Statistics South Africa
www.un.org/depts/unsd
The UN's statistics department

STOCK EXCHANGES
www.fibv.com
The International Federation of Stock Exchanges,
with links to member exchanges
www.liffe.com
London International Financial Futures and
Options Exchange
www.lme.co.uk
The London Metal Exchange
www.londonstockexchange.com
The London Stock Exchange
www.nasdaq.com
The Nasdaq
www.nyse.com
The New York Stock Exchange
www.tse.or.jp
The Tokyo Stock Exchange

TECHNOLOGY
www.business2.com
Home for *Business 2.0*, the tech industry's
thickest magazine
www.fastcompany.com
Fast Company, a tech-focused magazine
www.herring.com
Business news, technology and research for
investors and consumers
www.inside.com
E-zine on media and technology
www.news.com
Daily technology news from CNET
www.salon.com/tech
News, analysis and reviews from the stylish
Internet magazine *Salon*

www.slashdot.org
News for nerds in the know
www.theregister.co.uk
Cynical tech news, with a focus on Britain
www.thestandard.net
News, features and statistics about the Internet economy
www.upside.com
High-tech news and opinion
www.wired.com
The original tech-nerd mag

TRADE ASSOCIATION DIRECTORIES
ca.yahoo.com/Regional/Countries/
Canada/Business_and_Economy/
Organizations/Trade_Associations
Yahoo's directory of Canadian trade associations
dir.yahoo.com/Business_and_Economy/
Organizations/Trade_Associations
US and worldwide trade associations from Yahoo
www.martex.co.uk/taf/index.htm
The UK's Trade Associations Forum, which provides a meeting site for trade associations and A to Z links